Leading better Bible studies

Essential skills for effective small groups

Karen Morris and Rod Morris

AQUILA
PRESS

A book by Aquila Press

Published July 1997
Reprinted 1998, 2004, 2008, 2011
Copyright © Karen Morris and Rod Morris

Aquila Press is an imprint of Anglican Press Australia
PO Box A287, Sydney South, NSW 1235

National Library of Australia
ISBN 978-1-875861-35-4

Cover art by Joy Lankshear
Illustrations by Jenny Nisbet

Acknowledgments

Ada Lum, a staff worker with the International Fellowship of Evangelical Students, has spent many years training people to study the Bible. At a conference in May 1989, she challenged participants to take up the baton and continue the ministry of equipping people to read and understand God's word.

We were participants at that conference and this book represents our attempt to follow in the footsteps of those who have gone before. The ideas presented here have been gleaned from various sources over a number of years and where possible have been attributed to their original authors. However, at times we have not been able to remember the source of an idea and we apologise if we have not given credit where it is due.

Much of what you find written in these pages has been developed and refined over countless cups of coffee with colleagues, students, course participants and friends, and we would like to acknowledge their valuable contribution. In particular, we have benefited through ministering and working with our friends and colleagues at:

> The Anglican Education Commission of the Diocese of Sydney
>
> The Anglican Chaplaincy at Macquarie University, Sydney
>
> The Australian Fellowship of Evangelical Students
>
> St Barnabas' Anglican Church, Broadway, Sydney
>
> The Family Life Movement of Australia
>
> The School of Adult Education,
> University of Technology, Sydney
>
> Telecom Training Services.

We especially want to acknowledge the contribution, inspiration and support of Andrew and Heather Reid, Deb Sugars, Gerlinde and Ian Spencer, Andrew Newmarch, Michael Durrant, John Altmann, Anthea McCall and Brett Morgan who each read and commented on the manuscript, and Belinda Pollard who edited it for us.

To our parents and families, thank you for your love and support.

To Deb, John, Sarah, Kate and Emma, thank you for making us part of your family while we wrote this book.

Contents

4. Developing group life   105

5. Helping people pray   151

6. Sustaining group members   159

7. Continuing as a leader   189

Resources for Bible study group leadership   204

Preface

It is Bible study night and your group is due to arrive in fifteen minutes. It seemed like a good idea months ago when you agreed to lead, but now you're not so sure. You're tired, people don't seem nearly as enthusiastic as they did when the group first started, and you are wondering whether you really are the right person for the job. The Bible studies have been only average, and you are not sure how to improve them. You want people to know and love and trust Jesus more as a result of this group, but you are not sure how to make it happen!

Don't give up in despair. This book is for you. We both struggled with our first groups and were completely stressed out by our incompetence. We knew what we wanted to achieve, but had no idea how to get there. This book is the distillation of what we have learned. It includes a wide range of information we have acquired from theological training, adult education study and practice, practical group experience – and anywhere else we could find material! It has been written to enable you to lead more effectively.

People who are responsible for the functioning of Bible study groups have many different titles – facilitators, coordinators and so on. For convenience, we will talk about 'Bible study group leaders'. Throughout we refer to these leaders as participating in the group rather than being separate or ruling over group members.

Leading a Bible study group is great. Helping people to grow in their knowledge of God, building them up to be strong in their faith and assisting them as they study God's word is a very special privilege. To look back over the life of a group and see the changes that have occurred as people have learned from the Word of God is humbling and strengthening. However, it is also a great responsibility, not to be undertaken lightly. Those who teach and lead will be judged more harshly than others (James 3:1).

You lead as a coworker with God (1 Corinthians 3:5–9). You are a shepherd of the flock under your care and you are a model for them to imitate (1 Peter 5:1–5). Your leadership matters to God and to his people. Therefore, strive to lead well and seek to grow and develop as a leader. This book is written on the basis that you are seeking to grow and mature as a Christian so that you will be able to serve God to the best of your ability. We assume that leaders will have a **double purpose** in participating in a group. You will be **leading**

God's people, and **growing personally** as Christians. None of us should ask of group members more than we are prepared to do ourselves.

Bible study groups are a means to an end, and that end is to grow closer to God and more like his Son. We are passionate about helping people to hear of Jesus and to grow throughout their lives as a result of relating to him. We have been in groups where this has happened, and we want others to experience the joy of learning and growing and enjoying Bible study groups. Our prayer is that this book will enable you to lead better Bible studies.

Karen Morris and Rod Morris

Foundations

Balance is very important for a Bible study group leader. Some leaders focus on looking after people, and the groups that result are warm and friendly but do not concentrate on learning from God's Word. Other leaders focus on the Bible study component and completely ignore the personal needs of group members. This approach often results in the leader effectively giving a sermonette and the rest of the group being bored.

We have tried to remain balanced in our focus and include all the important aspects of a Bible study group. You might choose to read the chapters that seem most relevant to you; however, we think you would benefit from reading each section so that you consider all the aspects of leading a Bible study group.

To be thoroughly competent, a Bible study group leader needs to develop in the following seven areas:

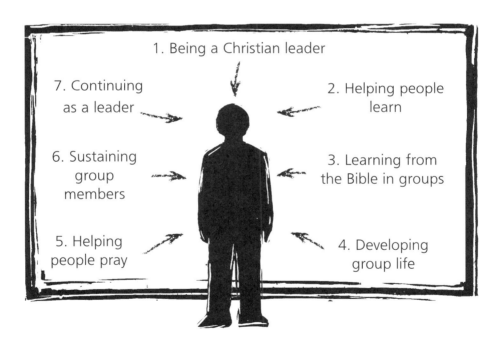

This does not imply that a Bible study group leader is incompetent if he or she is not expert in every area, it simply provides a guide for areas to work on.

Throughout the book are activities which enable you to reflect upon your own experience and consider some of the issues involved. These are flagged by the 'question mark' icon at left.

The seven sections of the book correspond with the seven parts of the model.

The first chapter is **Being a Christian leader**. This is the foundation of the rest of the book. We are working on two assumptions. The first is that leaders are men and women seeking to know God and serve him in their role as leaders. They trust in the saving work of our Lord Jesus Christ. The second assumption is that Christians study the Bible as a means to an end, and that end is to know God better as individuals. The way to understand God is primarily through Scripture, since that is how he has chosen to reveal himself to us.

On the basis of these two assumptions, this section of the book addresses the most significant aspects of leadership and explores the pitfalls that are possible if the nature of God's work is misunderstood.

The second chapter of the book is titled **Helping people learn**. Since our object in Bible study groups is to encourage the Christian growth of both ourselves and our group, through learning more about God and his work in history and in our world, we must do a good job of studying Scripture. To do this we must understand how people learn and how we as leaders can assist a person's learning. It is not enough simply to teach a topic. If there is to be any growth, the participants must learn.

The content of our teaching is so important that we must use the best possible methods to enable people to learn. Therefore this section examines basic adult education principles and the adult learning cycle, to enable leaders to accommodate various learning styles.

The third chapter, **Learning from the Bible in groups**, builds upon the first two. If the group leader is focusing on bringing people to a greater understanding of God through each person's different learning style, then he or she needs to handle the Bible well.

This section looks at the central core of the leader's task. We describe the nature of Bible study and how to write useful studies. We deal with technical aspects of studying the Bible as well as the practical aspects of helping people learn in a group setting. All of the work is based upon a biblical theology which is outlined in this section.

As young Bible study leaders, we desperately wanted a book to explain the possible techniques for studying the Bible. This section provides you with a list of Bible study techniques and supplies a sample study for each one.

The fourth chapter covers **Developing group life**. This section enables you to think about the nature of your group and how to bring people together in a way that promotes growth. We look at all stages of a group's development and discuss different models which shed light on the functioning of groups. We also deal with some of the roles people play and the problems which may be associated with these.

We have included a collection of ice-breaker and getting-to-know-you activities which will assist you in developing the life of your group.

Since the prayer life of a group is very important, the fifth chapter looks at **Helping people pray**. It is about helping people learn how to pray and then keep praying. It gives suggestions for making prayer time in your groups interesting and varied.

The sixth chapter addresses the issue of **Sustaining group members**. The previous chapters deal with looking after the group as a whole, while this one focuses on the individuals who make up your group. Once again, we look at the importance of the leader as a role model. We also include a discussion about helping people to be disciples.

Continuing as a leader is the focus of the last chapter. We encounter many people who have lead groups for twenty or thirty years, and we have included this section in an attempt to provide both encouragement and a way of continuing to learn even when you are highly skilled. We have also provided some thoughts about supervision for those who have many years of experience.

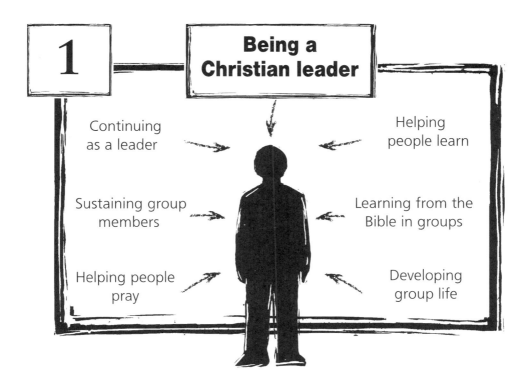

1 Being a Christian leader

- Continuing as a leader
- Helping people learn
- Sustaining group members
- Learning from the Bible in groups
- Helping people pray
- Developing group life

The starting point in training to lead Bible study groups is to develop a clear grasp of what it means to be a Christian leader. This is the foundation stone upon which everything else is assembled. It helps you determine your priorities, methods and constraints. To fly an aeroplane, you must understand the principles of aerodynamics. Failure to understand what a plane can do is at best foolish and at worst quite dangerous. Similarly, if you have misconceptions about Christian leadership, it will influence the whole of what you do as a Bible study group leader. It will distort your focus and priorities as a leader.

Which biblical principles have shaped your thinking about being a Christian leader?

As we conduct training we come across some common misconceptions: groups which meet regularly but don't actually study the Bible (these have lost sight of the centrality of Scripture); leaders who feel depressed when group members fail to meet expectations, or who manipulate people into some specified response (these have lost sight of the fact that God causes the growth); and study groups which approach Scripture with an academic detachment which does not modify the life of the group member (these have forgotten that Scripture demands change). You may have other misconceptions prevalent in your church or region.

The scriptural principles underlying Christian leadership can be summarised under seven headings:

> Christian leadership is God-given.
>
> Christian leadership is Christ-focused.
>
> Christian leadership is Spirit-empowered.
>
> Christian leadership is Word-centred.
>
> Christian leadership is prayerfully dependent.
>
> Christian leadership is life-exemplified.
>
> Christian leadership is change-demanding.[1]

Christian leadership is God-given

Paul regarded himself as a servant of Christ, entrusted with the secret things of God. He recognised that he must be faithful, and was aware that he would be judged by the Lord (1 Corinthians 4:1–4). In 1 Thessalonians 2:4 he writes 'just as we have been approved by God to be entrusted with the message of the gospel, even so we speak, not to please mortals, but to please God who tests our hearts'.

Peter also reminds us that the people we lead are entrusted to us. He writes 'tend the flock of God that is in your charge, exercising the oversight, not under compulsion but willingly, as God would have you do it – not for sordid gain but eagerly. Do not lord it over those in your charge, but be examples to the flock' (1 Peter 5:2–3).

Leadership is delegated to us by God and we are therefore accountable to him for how we exercise it. This principle has profound implications for us as leaders. While we may have pastors, priests or small group coordinators who supervise us, ultimately we are not responsible to them but to God.

---

1. This outline was developed from a course on Ministry, taught by the Rev. Keith Mascord of Moore Theological College, Sydney.

Christian leadership is Christ-focused

Christ is the centre. Paul reflects this when describing his own ministry: 'For I decided to know nothing among you except Jesus Christ, and him crucified' (1 Corinthians 2:2).

Jesus is not just the substance of Christian ministry – he is the goal. In Ephesians, Paul indicates that Christ-like maturity is the goal towards which the whole church is moving. He writes:

> The gifts he gave were that some would be apostles, some prophets, some evangelists, some pastors and teachers, to equip the saints for the work of ministry, for building up the body of Christ, until all of us come to the unity of the faith and of the knowledge of the Son of God, to maturity, to the measure of the full stature of Christ. We must no longer be children, tossed to and fro and blown about by every wind of doctrine, by people's trickery, by their craftiness in deceitful scheming. But speaking the truth in love, we must grow up in every way into him who is the head, into Christ... (Ephesians 4:11–15).

A number of years ago, we assembled a group of experienced Bible study group leaders to discuss leadership skills. Our conclusions were that Bible study group leaders need to:

✦ lead Bible input;

✦ facilitate group and individual prayer;

✦ provide pastoral care;

✦ promote personal evangelism;

✦ possess organisational ability;

✦ understand group dynamics; and

✦ possess oral communication skills.

On subsequent reflection, we realised this list lacked one major element. It does not set down the purpose of being a leader. It is impossible to lead effectively without a clear purpose in mind. The purpose directs how the leader's skills are used. A friend of ours often says that you can do all the right things, but if you don't have the ability to put them together in the right order and in the right proportions, then you are not really competent. A pile of bricks and a bag of mortar does not automatically result in a building.

Martin Bucer, the sixteenth century German reformer, decided the purpose of the pastor was:

1.   to draw to Christ those who are alienated.

2.   to lead back those who have been drawn away.

3.   to secure amendment of life for those who fall into sin.

4.   to strengthen weak and silly Christians.

5.   to preserve Christians who are whole and strong and urge them forward to the good.[2]

Although some of the language is quaint, we like this list. It focuses on moving people towards full maturity in Christ, whether they be committed Christians or people who don't yet know Jesus as their Lord. The purpose of the Bible study group leader is exactly this: to help people grow to maturity in Christ. While leadership involves doing all the things we listed on page 7, it is more than these alone. Leadership is Christ-focused and purposeful. Paul states: 'It is he whom we proclaim, warning everyone and teaching everyone in all wisdom, so that we may present everyone mature in Christ' (Colossians 1:28).

If the whole church is moving towards maturity in Christ, then Bible study groups and their individual members should also be moving in that same direction. The role of the group leader is to facilitate and guide the process; helping people grow in their relationship with Christ.

Christian leadership is Spirit-empowered

Without the work of the Spirit, leadership is simply human endeavour. The psalmist reminds us that 'unless the LORD builds the house, those who build it labour in vain. Unless the LORD guards the city, the guard keeps watch in vain' (Psalm 127:1). Throughout Scripture, we are reminded that it is God who gives understanding and brings people to new birth in Christ. Jesus states 'No one can come to me unless drawn by the Father who sent me ... they shall all be taught by God' (John 6:44–45). Paul tells us it is the Holy Spirit whom God has sent into our hearts who enables us to call God, 'Abba! Father!' (Galatians 4:6), and he reminds the Corinthians that

---

2.   M. Bucer, *Martini Bucer Opera Omnia Series 1: Deutsche Schriften*, Vol 7, 67-245 in D. Tidball, *Skilful shepherds* (Leicester: IVP, 1986), 47.

they are God's temple and that God's Spirit dwells in them (1 Corinthians 3:16). The work of the Spirit is the beginning of Christian faith. It is also instrumental in Christian growth.

Jesus promised his disciples that the Holy Spirit would guide them into all the truth (John 16:13). Paul reminds the Corinthians that he planted, Apollos watered, but God gave the growth. 'So neither the one who plants nor the one who waters is anything, but only God who gives the growth' (1 Corinthians 3:6–7).

Early this century, concert pianist Ignace Paderewski was Prime Minister of Poland. Among the stories that developed about him was one in which a woman took her son to a Paderewski concert to encourage the boy's progress on the piano. As they waited for the concert to begin, the mother began chatting to a friend and the boy wandered away bored. The lights dimmed and the curtain rose to reveal the boy playing 'Twinkle Twinkle, Little Star' on the grand piano. His mother was mortified, but at that moment the master appeared and whispered to the boy, 'Don't stop. Keep playing'. As the boy continued to play, the pianist reached around him and began to  add the most amazing accompaniment. Together they held the crowd absolutely rapt. It is like that with us and God. The Spirit's power converts our faltering attempts into a masterpiece. Don't stop, keep playing – even if it is only a nursery rhyme.

As with all ministry, Bible study group leadership is a spiritual battle. Paul reminds us our struggle is against 'the rulers, against the authorities, against the cosmic powers of this present darkness, against the spiritual forces of evil in the heavenly places' (Ephesians 6:12b). But we are not alone in the fight. As Paul tells Timothy, the Spirit is on our side. He writes 'guard the good treasure entrusted to you, with the help of the Holy Spirit living in us' (2 Timothy 1:14). The Spirit enables us to 'guard the treasure' by equipping us for works of ministry. Paul reminds the church

> there are varieties of gifts, but the same Spirit; and there are varieties of services, but the same Lord; and there are varieties of activities, but it is the same God who activates all of them in everyone. To each is given the manifestation of the Spirit for the common good (1 Corinthians 12:4–7).

9

As well as equipping us for ministry, the Spirit enables us to persevere at the task. Paul was able to write confidently 'I can do all things through him who strengthens me' (Philippians 4:13). He described his difficulties and struggles to the Corinthians, concluding 'we felt that we had received the sentence of death so that we would rely not on ourselves but on God who raises the dead' (2 Corinthians 1:9). It is as we rely on the God of the Resurrection that we engage in the task of leading a Bible study group.

Christian leadership is Word-centred

The fourth basic principle is a consequence of the first three. If leadership is God-given, Christ-focused and Spirit-empowered, then it follows that it should be centred on Scripture. God speaks through Scripture, we meet Christ in it and the Spirit illuminates it.

We learn about Jesus and come to believe in him through the Word. John wrote his Gospel 'so that you may come to believe that Jesus is the Messiah, the Son of God, and that through believing you may have life in his name' (John 20:31). Luke explains that his Gospel is recorded so that we may know the truth (Luke 1:4).

Paul clearly has a sense that ministry requires him to pass on this message of Christ. He writes: 'For I handed on to you as of first importance what I in turn had received...' (1 Corinthians 15:3a). Likewise, Paul urges Timothy to guard the gospel message (2 Timothy 1:13) and commission others who will faithfully pass it on: 'what you have heard from me through many witnesses entrust to faithful people who will be able to teach others as well' (2 Timothy 2:2).

As we meet together in our Bible study groups we continue in the tradition that Paul established. He asked Timothy to be faithful in handing on the message and now we receive it and do our part in the relay. We form part of the line who hand on the truth about Jesus down the ages. It is exciting to think that in years to come there will be those who look back on us as their spiritual forebears.

The psalmist finds a true perspective on life by meditating on the delights of God's word (Psalm 119); a practice that seems at risk of extinction in our current generation. Paul wrote to Timothy:

> continue in what you have learned and firmly believed, knowing from whom you learned it, and how from childhood you have known the sacred writings that are able to instruct

you for salvation through faith in Christ Jesus. All scripture is inspired by God and is useful for teaching, for reproof, for correction, and for training in righteousness, so that everyone who belongs to God may be proficient, equipped for every good work (2 Timothy 3:14–17).

Paul's point is clear: Scripture is central to Christian growth. Bible study groups without Scripture are an absurdity. Sailors who have ever lost a mast will agree that without a mast and sail there is no movement and certainly no joy. To conduct a Bible study without regularly studying the Bible is as ridiculous as trying to sail without a mast.

Therefore it is with great sadness (and some amazement) that we hear of Bible study groups which meet faithfully month after month, but no longer study the Scriptures. We have come across groups conducting 'Christian discussions'; others studying books by both Christian and secular authors; and yet others who have a time of worship. While each of these activities has some benefit for a Bible study group, alone they are inadequate. Scripture is essential in feeding the soul.

Christian leadership is prayerfully dependent

Prayer is crucial in Bible study group leadership. It is where we ask God to be about his business, as Paul demonstrates in his prayer for the Ephesians:

> I pray that, according to the riches of his glory, he may grant that you may be strengthened in your inner being with power through his Spirit, and that Christ may dwell in your hearts through faith, as you are being rooted and grounded in love. I pray that you may have the power to comprehend, with all the saints, what is the breadth and length and height and depth, and to know the love of Christ that surpasses knowledge, so that you may be filled with all the fullness of God (Ephesians 3:16–19).

Epaphras is a good example for us. Paul describes him in Colossians as 'always wrestling in his prayers on your behalf, so that you may stand mature and fully assured in everything that God wills' (Colossians 4:12). Wrestling in prayer for the people in our groups is part of recognising that it is God who is at work in the people whom we lead.

Christian leadership is life-exemplified

 Consider people who have had a big influence on you. Do you remember more about who they were or what they said?

This book is about ideas and methods for conducting a successful Bible study group. However, we need to say from the start that being a Christian leader is primarily about who you are, not what you do. Even though we spend the rest of this book discussing what you do, remember that the most significant part of leadership is being a faithful, godly, loving, integrated, repentant Christian. Without this, the rest is a waste of time.

Some of your attention needs to be devoted to developing your own character and godliness. Do not allow the tasks of ministry to overwhelm the heart of ministry – your own relationship with God. It is incredibly seductive to view ministry tasks as improving your relationship with God, but in fact they can destroy your relationship with him because you can hide behind lots of action and big talk. We have been devastated to see people finish their time in ministry and declare themselves no longer Christian.

In the business world, we are encouraged to look only at the individual's tasks and his or her ability to perform them. A business associate once commented: 'It doesn't matter what sort of person you are; all that matters is your ability to do the job!' While this may be adequate for business leadership (and personally we don't even accept that), who you are – your character, values and lifestyle – is crucial in your role as a Christian leader.

The leaders who had lasting impact on our Christian growth were godly people who were committed to studying Scripture and applying what they learned in order to live lives worthy of Christ. It isn't what they did that we remember ten years after the fact, it is who they were.

When conducting management development courses, we used a simple model called 'The Three Cs'. It asks if people are Competent to lead, if they are Committed to doing the task, and if they have the Confidence in themselves to take the initiative. However, when looking at Christian leadership, the model has grown to 'Six Cs and a

D'. We still look at competence, commitment and confidence, but we also believe it is important to consider character, convictions, content and dependence. This involves the following questions:

✦ **Character**
Are you the type of person you would like others to imitate?

✦ **Conviction**
Are you convinced about the centrality of Christ, faith and Scripture?

✦ **Content**
Are you able to handle the Bible appropriately?

✦ **Competence**
Do you have the skills to lead a group?

✦ **Commitment**
Are you committed to the wellbeing of the group?

✦ **Confidence**
Do you have the confidence to act as a leader?

✦ **Dependence**
Are you dependent on God in prayer?

 Spend some time answering each of these questions about yourself.

These questions reinforce the fact that ministry is about who you are as well as what you do. The difficulty is that the tasks are much easier than the holy life. New Testament writers recommend various tasks in Christian ministry, but the numbers of references to character and faith are often overlooked. It is significant that writers regularly urge people to godly behaviour rather than a particular set of tasks.

> We are putting no obstacle in anyone's way, so that no fault may be found with our ministry, but as servants of God we have commended ourselves in every way: through great endurance, in afflictions, hardships, calamities, beatings, imprisonments, riots, labors, sleepless nights, hunger; by purity, knowledge, patience, kindness, holiness of spirit, genuine love, truthful speech, and the power of God; with the weapons of righteousness for the right hand and for the left; in honor and

dishonor, in ill repute and good repute. We are treated as
impostors, and yet are true; as unknown, and yet are well
known; as dying, and see – we are alive; as punished, and yet
not killed; as sorrowful, yet always rejoicing; as poor, yet
making many rich; as having nothing, and yet possessing
everything (2 Corinthians 6:3–10).

Notice the personal characteristics mentioned, including: purity,
understanding, patience, kindness, sincere love, truthful speech,
genuineness.

The New Testament writers recognised that people would be
watching who they were. 'You know what kind of persons we proved
to be among you for your sake' writes Paul in 1 Thessalonians 1:5.
He tells the Philippians, 'Keep on doing the things that you have
learned and received and heard and seen in me' (Philippians 4:9).
The writer to the Hebrews likewise urges his readers to 'remember
your leaders, those who spoke the word of God to you; consider the
outcome of their way of life and imitate their faith' (Hebrews 13:7).

The knowledge that people are imitating you changes the way you
live. For example, it is easy to run out of time for the non-Christian
contacts you have had in the past. However, if you recommend
group members pray for non-Christian friends and then don't have
any of your own to pray for, your actions communicate louder than
your words.

This also applies to other spiritual disciplines such as reading your
Bible and praying. If you are not doing it, people will get the
message that you don't think it is important enough to waste your
precious time on. It may help to find a person who will study the
Bible with you and ask you about your life. Choose someone you
trust, someone capable of asking hard questions.

If you are new to leadership we suggest you find yourself a 'mentor',
who can support you and provide a good example for you. For us,
this is someone who 'we want to be like when we grow up'. Set up
regular meetings with your mentor and talk seriously about your
personal faith and life. Include all the aspects of your spiritual life,
your leadership and your personal growth. A great book to read
about these ideas is *Working the angles* by Eugene Peterson
(Michigan: Eerdmans, 1987).

Christian leadership is about mutual service rather than hierarchy.
Jesus is the ultimate model of this. He said 'whoever wishes to
become great among you must be your servant, and whoever wishes

to be first among you must be slave of all. For the Son of Man came not to be served but to serve, and to give his life a ransom for many' (Mark 10:43–45). Similarly, Paul tells the Romans that he is longing to see them 'so that I may share with you some spiritual gift to strengthen you – or rather so that we may be mutually encouraged by each other's faith, both yours and mine' (Romans 1:11–12). Notice the unusual combination of sharing a spiritual gift and being mutually encouraged. If you assume that the people you minister to also have something to teach you, you will listen more carefully and consider their point of view. It also makes it appropriate for you to ask them to pray for your current issues and share with them the crises of your life. All this results in mutual growth and encouragement.

Christian leadership is change-demanding

Our focus in leading a Bible study group is to help people become Christians and grow as believers. Our purpose is to bring about maturity in Christ, which is shown by changes in attitudes, beliefs and actions. We are not in the business of helping people simply acquire knowledge. If knowledge does not lead to action or changed lives then we need to ask why.

The great commandment is to love God and love our neighbour, so we expect this to be expressed as people faithfully live out their Christian lives. Discipleship involves the whole person, so Christian growth is expressed in all facets of life.

It is important to remember that a Bible study group is only part of the whole ministry of the church, and only part of an individual's experience as a Christian. While group participation can be a most significant influence on people, it will be a complement to other ministry activities and personal disciplines, including church, personal Bible reading, fellowship in other settings and prayer. These are all inputs into the spiritual life of an individual, as illustrated by the diagram on the following page.

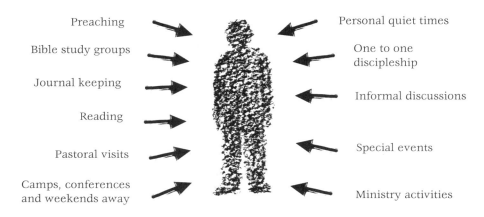

Preaching

Bible study groups

Journal keeping

Reading

Pastoral visits

Camps, conferences and weekends away

Personal quiet times

One to one discipleship

Informal discussions

Special events

Ministry activities

Our whole philosophy of ministry and particularly of small groups can be summed up by Paul's words to Timothy: 'Proclaim the message; be persistent whether the time is favourable or unfavourable; convince, rebuke, and encourage, with the utmost patience in teaching' (2 Timothy 4:2). The first part of the passage provides us with a clear task: proclaim the message. The second part gives us a brief on how to achieve the task: with utmost patience in teaching.

Our goal is to ensure that people are brought closer to Christ through contact with us. We want them to study the Bible and understand more about God and their relationship with him through Christ. Our process involves both knowledge and relationship. We need to teach and love people well, if they are to learn about God and his love for us demonstrated in Christ, which is our ultimate goal.

As a summary then: Do whatever you can to tell people about God and help them to grow. Be aware that who you are is as important as what you do and seek to grow personally in your relationship with God.

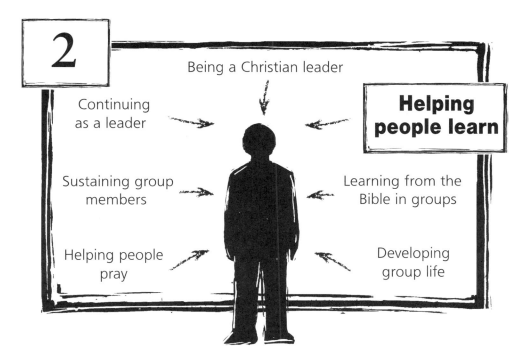

2

Being a Christian leader

Continuing
as a leader

Sustaining group
members

Helping people
pray

**Helping
people learn**

Learning from the
Bible in groups

Developing
group life

Have you ever had the experience of being in a Bible study group when something suddenly became blindingly clear? It is exhilarating for us as leaders to see this happen for others. Our most memorable occasion was when a member of one of our groups suddenly understood that being holy was not the same as legalism. These sudden leaps in understanding are our desire and our goal as leaders.

Helping people learn is crucial to Bible study group leading, and yet it is an area that many leaders have not reflected upon. In the past, much of what was written for Bible study groups was drawn from the disciplines of therapy and social work. While we recognise the helpful contribution these areas have made to group life, we have decided to focus our thinking in the field of adult education.

The reason for this is simple. We believe Bible study groups are primarily involved in the process of helping people learn from Scripture. While most groups will at times touch on deep personal issues and leaders will be involved in the pastoral care and support of people, their main task is to help people learn from the Bible.

Consider the following questions:

What were your most memorable learning experiences?

Who has helped you learn the most?

What things help you to learn?

What things keep you from learning?

In what ways is your approach to learning different from those around you?

Your answers to these questions will enable you to understand more about your own learning. People will answer these questions in different ways, reflecting their varying learning styles.

That people learn in different ways is one principle of adult education. This chapter explores adult education principles and suggests ways in which group leaders can use them to help in the process of learning. It is a foundation stone of our book. All the other chapters build upon these ideas. If you find the technical information hard to grasp at first, concentrate on the following sections:

✦   Principles of adult learning (page 21)

✦   The adult learning cycle (page 26)

✦   Individual learning styles (page 35)

These three sections provide most of the groundwork, and you can return to the other sections later.

The group member as a learner

There are three underlying principles to our adult Christian education philosophy:

1. Adult education is for the benefit of the learner

Many school children may be convinced that learning is only for the sake of their teacher, but nevertheless 'Learning is the duty and task of the learner'.[1] The reason we lead Bible studies is to help the other person learn, and the learning itself is an individual activity.

---

1.   D. Rockwell, 'Back to basics: Establishing and practising a learner-centred educational philosophy in the church', *Christian Education Journal* Vol IX, No 3 (1989), 15.

Another writer has said 'only learners themselves can learn and only they can reflect on their own experiences'.[2] This means that while we may lead a group, it is actually a collection of individuals who are each engaged in learning for themselves.

2. Each person's spiritual development is an individual process, between the person and God

We are all travellers together. Some may have progressed further than others and be able to provide helpful guidance and experienced advice, but none of us has 'arrived'. Bible study group leaders are learners alongside those they teach. We learn with and from our group members. We assist and guide them along the way, but ultimately their spiritual development is between them and God. We will be held accountable for the quality of our leadership, but they will be accountable for their response. We find this a great relief, since the temptation to feel responsible for another person's growth is quite strong.

3. Learning involves a fundamental shift or movement of mind

The process which leads to change within an individual is an enigmatic phenomenon. It is a complex concept which is more than the simple acquisition of knowledge or skills. It is a fundamental movement in our thinking. Sometimes this shift seems like trying to move a whale on dry land, at other times a minute detail can cause major change.

Learning is an active process which involves whole individuals and deals with the psychological, moral and intellectual dimensions within people. Learners engage in three steps:

✦ looking backwards to identify and examine the factors that govern their attitudes and actions;

✦ looking forward to predict the likely consequences and impact of their attitudes and actions; and

✦ identifying the feedback they receive in response to their attitudes and actions.

Once we understand that learning is a dynamic process, we are enabled to consider the possibility of intervening in order to enhance learning and facilitate this shift of mind.

---

2.   D. Boud, R. Keogh, and D. Walker, *Reflection: Turning experience into learning* (London: Kogan Page, 1985), 11.

19

The distinctive elements of adult Christian education

Is there a form of education which is distinctively Christian? One writer identifies the following differentiating features:

+ it is focused on God;

+ it is based on revelation;

+ it aims for personal transformation of the whole person.[3]

These theological truths provide the framework for a model of adult Christian education. The Bible is foundational to Christianity; spiritual growth and development is achieved by personal understanding and application of Scripture. We have already determined that facilitating Christian growth is our main goal as leaders. The primary purpose of adult Christian education, then, is to enable people to learn from the Bible so that they can make sense of the world in which they live and relate to the Lord who is sovereign over it.

The important role of experiencing Scripture

Emerson wrote in *The American scholar,* 'Only so much do I know, as I have lived'.[4] Most educational writers acknowledge a correlation between learning and the individual experience of the learner. In 1938, long before current theories of adult education emerged, John Dewey stated: 'All genuine education comes about through experience'.

It is not true, however, that all experience results in learning. Experience does not equal learning any more than 'simply sawing a bow across violin strings will make a violinist'.[5] Dewey states that 'it is a certain quality of practice ... which produces the expert and the artist'.[6] A particular type of directed and purposeful experience is required.

Therefore, while it is safely assumed that genuine learning requires

---

3. H. Hendricks, 'What makes Christian education distinct' in E. Palmer, R. Hestenes, H. Hendricks, *Mastering Teaching* (Portland: Multnomah, 1991).

4. Lewis C. Henry, *5000 quotations for all occasions* (Philadelphia: Blakiston, 1945), 81.

5. R. Archambault, (Ed) *John Dewey on education* (Chicago: University of Chicago Press, 1964), 201.

6. Archambault, 201.

experience, the type and the impact of an experience must be considered. For Bible study groups, this point is extremely important. **It is not enough to meet for Christian discussion. What we must have is a genuine experience of engaging with God's Word.** Christian learning happens as we engage with God's revelation of himself. Reading, listening to, reflecting on and discussing Scripture are all elements of the experience of a Bible study group. It is this experience of God's self-revelation which is the basis of true learning.

Principles of adult learning

Over twenty years ago, Malcolm Knowles proposed a series of principles defining the way adults learn. Knowles' principles have since become accepted as foundational in the field of adult education. One of the interesting side effects of his work is that his proponents have realised children also learn best in education based upon his principles. Knowles proposed that:

1. As people mature, their self-concept moves from one of being a dependent personality towards one of being a self-directing human being.

2. They accumulate a growing reservoir of experience that becomes an increasing resource for learning.

3. Their readiness to learn becomes oriented increasingly towards fulfilling roles and responsibilities in society.

4. Their time perspective changes from one of postponed application to one of immediate application; their orientation of learning changes from subject- to problem-centredness.[7]

Each of these principles has profound implications for the way we deal with people in our groups. To illustrate these principles we will introduce two typical adult learners. Anne is single and Peter is married. They work at demanding jobs during the week and attend Bible study on Thursday night and church on Sunday. They have not studied for many years and have many relationships to which they are committed.

The first principle is: As Anne and Peter mature, their self-concept

---

7. P. Jarvis, *Adult and continuing education* 2nd ed. (London: Routledge, 1995), 90–94.

moves from one of being dependent personalities towards one of being self-directing human beings.

Anne and Peter want to be involved in the decision-making about the direction of their learning. There needs to be a consultative process when the group is determining its direction and activities.

They also want to be able to 'get their hands dirty' in any learning they do. Therefore, the leader's aim is to involve Anne and Peter as much as possible in the actual process of learning. Rather than doing all the research ourselves and then presenting them with our fully formed views, as leaders we should be enabling them to work things out for themselves. As one writer has said: 'Instead of spoon-feeding truth to people, I have to … risk giving them the spoon, letting them discover the satisfying taste of the gospel'.[8]

We identify two types of group leaders: 'safari guides' and 'tour guides'. The Castles of Europe tour guide spends a long time going around Europe picking out the best castles, doing the research and determining what people should see. He or she produces a package tour which is fixed and inflexible in structure.

In contrast, the African safari guide has a general idea where the group might go, but the group is involved in the decision-making. Group members come with some knowledge, inspect maps and ask questions. They also clean, pack up tents and load trucks. The guide is there to keep them safe, point out dangers and pitfalls, and generally maintain the group.

We believe Bible study group leaders need to be African safari guides rather than Castles of Europe tour guides. We need to work out how to involve people in the whole process of learning rather than present them with a fully formed package. The Bible is not something to be looked at through the windows of a tour bus – it requires involvement and participation.

When it comes to learning, Anne and Peter want help and they want to be active rather than passive. They learn best when they can be involved in the action. They are self-directing and appreciate the opportunity to learn for themselves rather than being told what to think. In the next chapter you will see how we have incorporated this principle into Bible study techniques.

---

8. E. Palmer, 'Teaching through preaching' in E. Palmer, R. Hestenes, and H. Hendricks, *Mastering teaching* (Portland, Oregon: Multnomah Press, 1991), 95.

The second principle is this: Anne and Peter accumulate a growing reservoir of experience that becomes an increasing resource for learning.

This experience provides a framework into which new information can be integrated; it acts as a standard against which insights are checked; and it acts as a barrier if they refuse to consider areas about which they have already reached conclusions!

Adults accumulate knowledge and become expert in some areas. Of course, this does not mean that Anne and Peter know everything, or that they don't need to be taught things they do not yet understand. Rather, it means that we lead a group in a way that helps them make use of this reservoir of experience and avoid its pitfalls.

> **The Bible is not something to be looked at through the windows of a tour bus – it requires involvement and participation.**

We have already established that a Bible study group is a group of Christian brothers and sisters who join together to study Scripture and help each other grow into Christian maturity. They meet together as peers, even though some may have greater knowledge and understanding than others. Their greater knowledge is utilised as a resource for the group, as they share their insights for the benefit of all. As leaders, we use our knowledge and understanding as a safety net to ensure that the group does not fall into error or miss significant aspects of a passage as we work on it together.

This principle does not always have the impact it should on our leadership styles. If we valued Anne's and Peter's experience then we would always treat them with respect. We would assume they were capable of working out information rather than being told. We would expect them to be as responsible in the group as they are in other parts of their life. We would try to help them make connections between their experience and the knowledge we are introducing, while also asking them to reconsider areas which need to be modified in the light of Scripture.

Imagine that Anne is an Engineer and Peter a Nursing Sister. We might assume that Anne has some experience with arranging information into flow-charts or drawing models in conceptual form. We could ask the group to look at some aspect of Scripture, such as Paul's argument explaining the use of gifts for the building up of the church in Ephesians 4, and use Anne's expertise to help us devise a model for it. (This will be explained further in Chapter 3.) Similarly, we might assume that Peter would understand dealing with people and the nature of conflict resolution. We could draw on his experience when it came to applying the Bible in our relationships, and when helping the group deal with interpersonal problems. (Conflict will be discussed further in Chapter 6.) These are just a couple of ways to make use of Anne's and Peter's reservoirs of experience.

The third principle is: Anne's and Peter's readiness to learn becomes oriented increasingly towards fulfilling roles and responsibilities in society.

This change from child to adult is most noticeable once people can make choices about their education. Information for the sake of information is not necessarily a compelling reason for Anne and Peter to learn. In our observation, almost all adult students expose themselves to education for a purpose. Anne might be trying to improve her working skills, Peter might be trying to get a job he would prefer, or they might want to be more effective in their relationships. Anne may choose to learn to sail as a means of exercise or recreation, while Peter may attend a course on Spanish cooking as an opportunity to make new friends. People participate in learning for an array of reasons.

This is also true of Christians. We learn because we think we have a need for this information. Therefore, if we want to encourage our group members in learning, we must be able to communicate the reason for learning and understanding this information. If we can relate their learning to their spiritual life, their social roles and responsibilities, their relationships and their work then they will be more inclined to learn. Starting a Bible study by saying that we are going to look at the rebuilding of the temple in Ezekiel may not establish a need to learn for an adult. Alternatively, we could say we are going to study how to respond to God in our lives, an issue which is relevant to all of us.

The fourth principle builds upon the others: Anne's and Peter's time perspective changes from one of postponed application to one of immediate application; their orientation of learning changes from subject- to problem-centredness.

Anne and Peter require short-term gains. They need to know they are actually achieving something and will gain from it. They want to be living well as believers and growing in their faith and love for Jesus. They are particularly interested to know: 'What difference will this make to me this week?' If we answered this question every week, we would be encouraging people's learning. Therefore our Bible studies should aim to change lives and promote action as a result of the things learned.

This means that Bible studies must always involve considering how to apply what we learn to daily life. Sometimes people assume they can only really study the epistles, since they do not know how to apply some of the other parts. Our view is that all parts of the Bible should be studied over time, and therefore the group as a whole must develop skills in how to apply it. This simply means harder work. It requires the group and the leader to work hard to learn and understand even difficult sections.

Allan Rogers has also produced a set of principles for adult education which add to those of Knowles. Rogers writes:

✦ Participation is voluntary (not necessarily attendance).

✦ Participation is purposeful.

✦ Experience and values will differ in any group.

✦ Learners will have definite expectations of what they will learn and how they will learn it.

✦ All adult learners have competing demands and interests.

✦ Learners have preferred learning styles.[9]

Participation is voluntary implies that adults can withdraw their participation at any time. Rogers notes that attendance is not always voluntary. Anne and Peter may attend your group because they are expected to, but they might choose not to participate.

Participation is purposeful is similar to Knowles' third principle of learning with a goal in mind or a problem to solve. The group will want to know why they should bother. If you want long-term commitment then you need a convincing reason. Anne and Peter lead busy lives and the commitment to their group is time-consuming, therefore they will want to know if it is worth the effort.

Experience and values will differ in any group relates to the changes adults go through as they acquire experience. This is clear with Anne and Peter since they are skilled in different areas and

9.   Quoted in 'Adult Learning': Associate Diploma in Adult Education Course Notes, (University of Technology, Sydney/Deakin University/Telecom Training Services, Geelong, 1993).

consider different things to be important. They are competent in their own fields, and they bring that with them to the group. This is an extension of the 'reservoir of knowledge' concept outlined in Knowles' second principle.

Learners will have definite expectations of what they will learn and how they will learn it. This principle is not mentioned in Knowles' list. Rogers includes it because he recognises that adults turn up to a group with expectations in mind. They may not divulge these expectations but they do exist. Anne and Peter came to their group expecting to build good relationships and to learn more about the Bible. They thought that this might be boring because the leader was going to give them a mini-sermon each week, but were pleasantly surprised when they had to get involved.

This leads on to the next principle. **All adult learners have competing demands and interests.** The people in your group probably have busy jobs, are studying or looking for work and all have commitments to families, friends and other groups. Therefore attending Bible study has to be worth the effort. Leaders need to work hard to make it so.

The final principle is that **learners have preferred learning styles**. We highlighted this with the questions you considered at the beginning of this chapter. People like different sorts of activities and they absorb information in different ways. One writer has said 'Sometimes I forget that if I don't teach in such a way that the students actually learn something, I'm wasting my precious breath and their fidgety time.'[10] This is especially true of leading Bible study groups. We will return to consider learning styles in more detail later in this chapter, but first we will consider a process of learning that is common to all.

The adult learning cycle

We are currently in the process of preparing for overseas missionary service. We have begun the process of packing up everything and trying to decide what to take and what to leave behind. We are also trying to understand a new culture. How will we communicate? What will make sense? What won't? We need to know how to communicate in a way that helps others understand and respond.

---

10.   P. Zettler, 'Not everyone learns alike' *Leadership*, Vol. 8, No. 3 (1987) 28–33.

This is obvious when entering a new culture, but sometimes forgotten in our own.

A fundamental premise of ministry is that **because what we teach is so important, we must use the best possible process in order to help people learn it.**

The adult learning cycle seeks to explore and explain the way adults learn. It has profound implications for us as we seek to minister to people, and can greatly enhance our ability to communicate with those we teach.

Adult learning researcher David Kolb recognised that learning is a process of cycling through a number of stages, with each stage important to the overall process. He depicted the process of learning with the following diagram, where each of the stages impacts upon the following one.

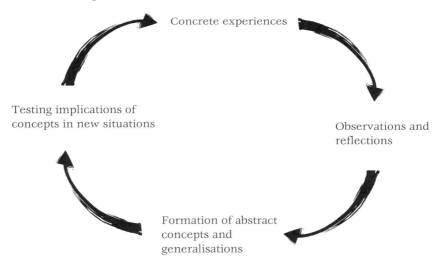

Concrete experiences

Observations and reflections

Formation of abstract concepts and generalisations

Testing implications of concepts in new situations

The first stage is the one in which a person has some sort of experience. It may be intellectual or physical; listening to a sermon or falling off a bike. The particular experience we are concerned about is for individuals within the group to have a personal encounter with God's revelation of himself. That is, we want people to have an experience of Scripture.

Within the model, experience is the input which generates learning, but we have already seen that experience by itself does not equate with learning. We noted that the type of experience and its impact affected whether learning took place. Now we turn our attention to the learner. It is possible to have heaps of experience and learn nothing from it! Have you met people who never seem to learn from experience – they simply repeat the same behaviour *ad infinitum*.

Having had an experience, a person needs to notice it in order to learn from it. One writer in adult education has said, 'an experience which isn't noticed is just another happening'[11]. Noticing provides the data for further reflection. **One of the primary roles of a leader is to help people notice what they might otherwise overlook.**

A dilemma can draw a learner's attention to the issues requiring consideration. For example, prior to the heart attack your friend could not tell you anything about cholesterol, exercise or arteries, but after a brush with death he or she became the fount of all knowledge.

Some researchers believe that 'learning must be based on the discovery or surfacing of dilemmas'.[12] However, this assumes that there is no learning to be gained from examining the expected and predictable, an assumption which others regard as unwise.[13] Individuals can benefit from reflecting on both the surprising and the expected. While dilemmas facilitate the process of reflection by focusing attention sharply onto issues, reliance on dilemma alone could easily lead to learning which is purely reactive. Therefore the learner needs to develop ways of noticing the expected and predictable, as well. **We need to notice the surprises in Scripture and the things we already know to be true.**

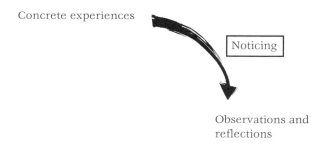

Concrete experiences

Noticing

Observations and reflections

To learn from experience we need to move onto the second phase of the cycle, actually reflecting upon the experience. This involves making a point of noticing the experience and spending some time

11. M. Horton, J. Kohl, and P. Kohl, *The long haul* (New York: Doubleday, 1990).
12. C. Argyris, and D. Schon, *Theory in practice: Increasing professional effectiveness* (San Francisco: Jossey Bass, 1974), 99.
13. P. Jarvis, *Adult and continuing education: Theory and practice* (London: Croom Helm, 1983), 60.

thinking about it. Reflection means asking questions about it, trying to work out the causes and the effects. It involves looking at an experience from differing angles and perspectives, seeking to understand what happened or what was said. It means listening to other people's reactions and analysing them in light of your own.

From the reflection phase you move into making theories about the experience.

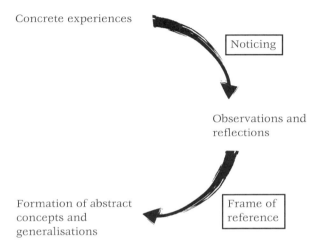

This phase involves spending time working out theories which make sense of the experience and others like it. This requires forming abstract concepts and generalisations, rules and principles which explain the experience and can be applied to future events. This is also the point at which we draw on the things we already know – our 'reservoir of experience' – which act as a frame of reference for our new experience. This is the lens through which we consider the new experience.

Attributing meaning to the experience is crucial. Merely observing an event such as falling off a bicycle is not sufficient. The learner must interpret, define and work out the significance of what he or she has noticed. This is especially true of reading Scripture. The meaning given to a particular piece of information depends upon the way it is combined with other pieces of information. The validity of what is learned depends on the interpretations drawn. The association between new and old knowledge and attitudes can lead to discovery and growth. Combining the new with the old results in challenge, re-assessment and modification of existing attitudes, understanding, beliefs and actions.

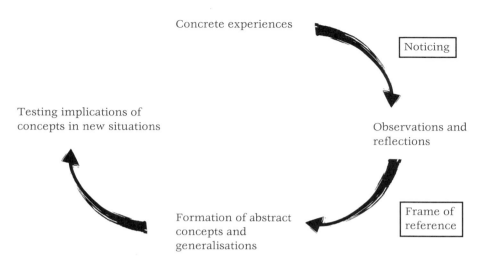

The final stage is one in which a person makes plans about how to behave or react differently on the basis of these new theories. This requires the application of newly-devised theories to real situations and circumstances. At this point in the cycle, the person has moved beyond simply thinking and is now engineering different conditions under which the new situation might arise. Consequently when another experience arises it is felt as a new experience, under different conditions, and this then prompts another trip around the learning cycle. We remember the model in this abbreviated form:

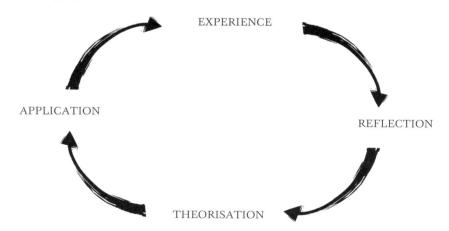

The following story illustrates the stages of the learning cycle. As we explain it, follow the diagram.

When Rod was a young driver, he had a near-accident in his car. He was driving on a wet road and was not very experienced. As he came into a small country town, he realised he was doing 100 km per hour rather than 60, so he braked suddenly to slow down. However, he also happened to be taking a slight turn in the road. The car skidded on the wet surface of the corner, spun 180°, and careered across the oncoming lane and onto the shoulder of the road.

This was the initial **experience** in Rod's learning. When the car finally stopped, he sat and wondered why it had happened. The rapid heartbeat and the fact that he was on the wrong side of the road facing backwards meant he had to notice that something had gone wrong. Was there something wrong with the steering? Was there something wrong with the brakes? Was it possible that he himself had done something wrong? All these questions went through his mind as he sat shaken but unhurt. This was the start of the **reflection** stage.

When he got home, he explained the situation to his Dad, who told him about the effects of heavy braking on wet corners. It seemed to make sense, although Rod was pretty keen to blame some peculiarity of the car. At this point, his Dad was providing additional information for his frame of reference. He was helping him in the process of forming theories regarding travelling on wet roads. Rod made some conclusions and decided that he should adjust his driving style. This was the **theorisation** stage.

However, he did not progress beyond theorisation to application, and a couple of months later the same thing happened. He returned to the first stage of the cycle – **experience**. This time he went through the learning process a lot more quickly. He understood what had happened and why. There was added impetus in his learning this time as he had just passed a semi-trailer and he realised he could easily have ended his young life at that point. Contrary to his previous experience, this time he went through every step of the learning process and adjusted his driving style – the **application** stage. It was at this point that you could say he had learned from the experience.

The evidence that he had learned was that the **experience** did not happen again, even under similar conditions.

To summarise, learning is a process which involves a number of steps. It is a series of moves towards a desired goal. In our case, the goal is to understand Scripture and apply it to our lives. Each step involves assessment and evaluation which shapes the next step. Learners are constantly changing. Each experience strengthens, redefines or challenges the conclusions previously made. Meaning is integrated into the learner's structure, providing him or her with a foundation for further experience.

Bible study groups and the learning cycle

The learning cycle described by Kolb is fundamental to Bible study groups. The individual still learns individually. The learner within the context of a group needs to engage in the same learning processes as he or she would as an individual learner. The group enhances the process. Dewey suggested as a general principle that 'growth is furthered in any branch of human undertaking by contact with the accumulated and sifted experiences of others'.[14]

This is how the learning cycle works in a Bible study group. First, we help people **experience** God's word. This does not mean 'telling' them, but getting people to engage with Scripture for themselves. We also need to work out ways for getting people to notice Scripture – to see what is in front of their eyes. We prompt people to ask their own questions of the text, because they are more likely to notice the answer when they are asking the question.

Next, we give people time and assistance to **reflect** upon what they are reading. Some people find reflecting easy, but for many, thirty seconds is a long silence. The sort of things we do to help people reflect include getting them to write and asking them to talk in pairs.

Having reflected, we help people draw conclusions and principles from Scripture – the **theorising** process. This will also involve providing any information people need to understand correctly their reflections. We provide the frame of reference information which the learner may not have, but which is essential for properly understanding the experience. Getting people to form a group opinion or argue for a particular view is helpful here.

Finally, we complete the learning cycle by helping people **apply** these conclusions and principles to the way they live. This is when learning can truly be said to have taken place. We are surprised when we hear sermons which fail to apply the passage to daily life. The preacher, having done so much work on exegesis and hermeneutics, fails to complete the learning cycle. In ministry, our task as educators is to help people through the whole of the learning cycle, not just the first three stages.

14. Archambault, 150.

These steps are crucial in the process of facilitating learning. They help people from the initial stage of engaging with Scripture all the way through to applying what they have learned, resulting in changed lives.

The Bible study group leader is required to manage the group so that learning is enhanced through interaction with others. When we interact in a group, our perspective and the meaning we attribute is challenged, and we receive feedback which allows us a better understanding of each experience. However, these interactions have the potential to be both positive and negative. As leaders, we want to encourage exchanges which are helpful for learning. How to manage these interactions for the good of everyone in the group is discussed in Chapter 4: 'Developing group life'.

Leaders provide support, encouragement and motivation for learning. Learning is hard work, and as leaders we seek to help people persevere.

The leader as a facilitator

Recently Karen helped at the birth of a friend's baby. She attended the birth classes, watched the videos, read the books and turned up on the big day. During the labour she massaged the mother's back, fed her ice, mopped her brow (yes, seriously) and got food when it was needed. The whole process was long and hard but she knew at the end there would be a baby and it would be worth it. Karen was facilitating the birth of the baby.

The leader's role is to facilitate learning. Facilitators of learning aid, abet, assist, empower, enable, ease, expedite, help, promote, support, and reassure the learner and the learning process. They do not alter the process which the learner must undergo in order to learn, they merely facilitate it. The primary role for any facilitator of learning must be to assist the learner as he or she progresses through the learning cycle. Facilitators intervene in the process of noticing, interpreting and applying in order to enhance the learning gained.

Let us clarify here that we do not simply mean keeping people happy, a misapprehension which some Christians hold. **Facilitation is more than helping the group have a 'good discussion', and facilitation does not mean the group can hold any opinion it likes, regardless of its validity.**

We use facilitation with its technical meaning:

> The facilitator regulates the group's activities by modelling, questioning, clarifying, reinforcing (or not reinforcing), reflecting feelings, making process comments at the intrapersonal, interpersonal, and group levels, teaching, linking, summarising, confronting, and giving feedback … In short, the facilitator chooses from a broad repertoire of skills those that will have the most beneficial effect on the activity of the group into which he or she wishes to intervene. Implicit is the assumption the most beneficial intervention may be no intervention, and the facilitator needs to develop a sense of where this is the most effective way of regulating.[15]

Facilitation is the process of helping the group move to a fuller understanding of the truth. **The point of Bible study is to bring out the truth.** We are not creating truth, truth is there through revelation in Scripture. We are helping the group understand that revelation by bringing the truth to light.

There are a number of ways for leaders to facilitate the learning cycle. We can promote the development of a conducive learning environment. We can provide skills and strategies for learning. We can supply feedback which helps learners to notice an experience. We can question their intentions and underlying assumptions. We can create opportunities for learners to intervene in their own learning. We can encourage reflection and attention to feelings. We can instigate opportunities for further learning and provide the insight and perspective of a critical friend.

As facilitators of learning, we do everything possible to help people through the learning cycle. Our role is like that of a midwife. We are in the process of bringing the truth to birth in the lives of group members. We do everything possible to help people understand the truth.

---

15. L. Anderson and S. Robertson, 'Group facilitation', *Small group behaviour,* Vol 16 No 2 (May 1985), 152.

Individual learning styles

Individuals have a preference for particular stages of the learning cycle. This preference is referred to as a 'learning style'. Let's revisit the model to remind us of the important points.

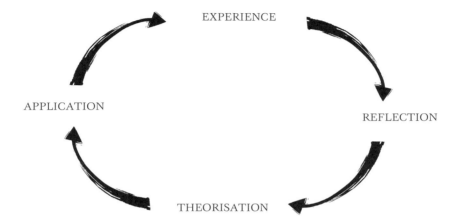

Some people enjoy the initial stage of learning: generating experience. These people are called **activists.** They love the 'doing' part of learning. They enjoy the challenge of something new and fresh.

Others prefer the reflection stage. They enjoy the opportunity to reflect and consider how various things relate. They like looking for patterns, comparing experiences and considering an experience from various perspectives. These people are **reflectors.**

Other learners, the **theorists,** prefer the theorisation stage. They like formulating explanations and developing principles. They enjoy making all the various facts and ideas fit into one coherent theory.

Others still prefer to focus on the end results of the whole process. They like knowing the consequences, and ask 'What difference does it make?' They enjoy having a list of actions and things to do. Their concern is real-life application. They are aptly called **pragmatists.**

These learning styles can be added to the earlier diagram. See the example on the following page.

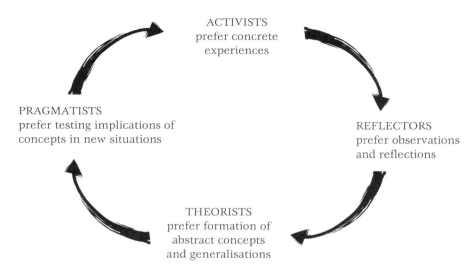

Imagine you have purchased a new stereo. It is sitting in your lounge room in all six of its boxes waiting to be assembled. Each of the preferences will deal with this situation differently. The activists will rip open all the boxes, plug in all the leads and turn it on, hoping that it won't blow up. Theorists, on the other hand, will read all the manuals and perhaps even a book on electronics before assembling the equipment. Pragmatists will also read the manual, although they will only read the parts they aren't familiar with. They will work out what they need to know to achieve the task and then put it together. Reflectors will think about the task for a long time. They may even make a cup of tea and ring their mothers. Eventually a frustrated activist will put it together for them. This is a caricature of each type but it gives you some idea of the different preferences.

We have listened to many preachers, and the best are effective because they manage to accommodate each of the learning style preferences within their preaching. Evangelicalism tends to favour theorists and reflectors, so we need to work especially hard at helping the activists and pragmatists learn from what we teach. This means ensuring that activists have something to do and think about, and a clear sense of progress, while pragmatists require tangible outcomes to apply in their lives.

Learning style preferences have similar implications for Bible study group leadership. A group of more than six people generally contains a representative of each learning style preference. You do not have to find out what learning style people prefer. Simply recognise that the group will include people who learn differently to you, and learn to accommodate each style within a session.

Facilitators of learning tend to teach and lead others in the way that they like to learn. It is easy to be excited about the content of a topic and believe that you are doing a brilliant job teaching it to others, while totally missing the majority of your audience. The solution is deliberately to check that you are moving through the learning cycle to ensure that you are catering to the learning styles of your audience.

Each learning style has its own dangers. A couple are worth noting for Bible study groups. Activists easily become bored with traditional comprehension questions, and study series which go more than six weeks. Reflectors can get left behind and then frustrate others by raising issues discussed ten minutes ago. Theorists can get bogged down in minute details and pragmatists can become very frustrated in a group which never arrives at an outcome. Activists, theorists and pragmatists create space for themselves. In fact, it is often difficult to keep them quiet. Reflectors however tend to withdraw in order to think. This means they will often struggle in a Bible study group as they get left behind. Therefore, the leader has to create space for them to reflect and also provide an avenue for them to re-enter the discussion and contribute their thoughts.

We must ensure we do not devalue other people's learning style preferences, especially when we are considering who to train as future leaders. We often notice potential leaders because they are on our wavelength, but this can mean that godly, able individuals are overlooked. We have administered learning styles questionnaires with various groups of clergy and lay Bible study group leaders. The common theme has been a high number of theorists and reflectors, and a low number of activists and pragmatists. (The exception was a community church which had a high number of activists and pragmatists.) We particularly noticed this pattern because we used to work with a telecommunications company where the groups were more evenly spread across all the learning styles. This strong pattern suggests two potential problems: we may be missing a significant portion of the population by teaching in a way which fails to recognise various learning style differences; and we may be developing a self-perpetuating focus on theorists and reflectors.

The following books are helpful if you wish to read further about applying these principles to ministry:

> H.G. Hendricks and W.D. Hendricks, *Living by the Book* (Chicago: Moody Press, 1991).

> P. Honey and A. Mumford, *Using your learning styles* (Berkshire: Maidenhead, 1986).

> Anton Baumohl, *Making adult disciples* (Homebush West: Anzea, 1984), specifically the chapter 'How learning occurs'.

Without good content, the educational task is meaningless and futile, for content is the very heart of our message. But without good process, we undermine our work and limit our effectiveness. Our hope is that you will work hard at having both good content and good process; a process which both works through the learning cycle and accommodates individual learning style preferences.

How people absorb information

As well as their individual learning styles, people also have preferences for how they absorb information. Everyone absorbs information in three ways – by seeing, by hearing, and by doing – but most people have a preference for one method above the others. The technical terms for these are **visual**, **auditory** and **kinaesthetic**. Visual learners prefer to see something as they seek to understand it, auditory learners like to have it explained clearly and precisely, and kinaesthetic learners need to do it before they feel they have fully mastered it. People have a preference for one or two of these which affects how they assimilate and express ideas. This will influence their approach to the learning cycle. At each stage, a visual person will want to see information, while an auditory will be happy to hear it, and a kinaesthetic will want to be 'doing something'.

The following example illustrates this concept.

When a person says the word 'apple', some people:

✦   see an apple – red and glossy;

✦   hear the word apple and repeat the sounds, listening to the phonetics of the word;

✦   feel the texture of an apple – smooth, firm and weighty.

Your response to this example may suggest your own preference for visual, auditory or kinaesthetic input. The short quiz on the next page will help you identify your preferences. As you are simply describing yourself, there is no best answer for these questions. (Later in this chapter you will learn how to use this knowledge of yourself to improve your leadership practice.)

In a Bible study group, you might notice which preference is strongest for people by the way they talk. People operate on more than one channel, but tend to favour one or two over the others.

Visual learners may say:

I see what you mean.

I saw red.

The crowd all stood and clapped.

Auditory learners may say:

That sounds right to me.

I heard warning bells.

There was thunderous applause.

Kinaesthetic learners may say:

I feel comfortable with that.

That just turned me right off.

Everyone was really moved.

Visual/auditory/kinaesthetic preferences

Please circle your most preferred answer.

	Visual	Auditory	Kinaesthetic
When you spell, do you	write it to see if it 'looks right'?	use the 'sounding it out' approach?	write it to find out if it 'feels right'?
When you concentrate, do you	get distracted by untidiness?	get distracted by noise?	get distracted by movement?
When you are meeting people, do you	forget names but remember faces?	forget faces but remember names?	remember best what you did together?
When you contact people, do you	prefer a direct personal meeting, face to face?	prefer the telephone?	talk while walking or during another activity?
When you are relaxing, do you	prefer to watch TV/read/see a play?	prefer to listen to the radio/play CDs?	prefer to play games or sport?
When you enjoy the arts, do you	like painting?	like music?	like dancing?
When you try to interpret someone's mood, do you	primarily look at facial expression?	listen for the tone of voice?	watch body movements?
When you are reading, do you	like descriptive scenes that you can visualise?	enjoy dialogue, conversation, and well-constructed phrases?	prefer action stories or are not a keen reader?
When you learn, do you	like to see posters, diagrams, slides, demonstrations?	like verbal instructions, talks and lectures?	prefer direct involvement, activities and tasks?
Total	V:	A:	K:

We tend to assume that people learn (and enjoy learning) in the same way we do. This can result in Bible studies prepared predominantly for visual learners or auditory learners or kinaesthetic learners, thereby limiting the learning that takes place.

For example, Karen tends to draw diagrams, flow-charts, illustrations – she 'shows' people what she means. When questioning their grasp of concepts she asks them 'Do you see what I'm talking about?' Karen caters for visual learners automatically, but must make a deliberate effort to assist auditory and kinaesthetic learners. To accommodate other preferences, she must explain information in a variety of ways and/or get the group members to do something. To ask a question in a way that an auditory or a kinaesthetic learner will understand, she needs to rephrase her questions: 'Does that sound right?' or 'How does that feel?' She also needs to allow group members the opportunity to hear information rather than simply reading for themselves as she likes to do.

Our Bible study group meetings need to be visually stimulating (something to look at), auditorially stimulating (something to listen to) and kinaesthetically stimulating (something to do). The traditional approach of sitting in a circle and discussing questions fails to engage both the visual and the kinaesthetic learner.

These principles have implications for group communication. In Bible study groups, people need to feel understood. They will be more inclined to contribute and participate if the leader 'speaks their language'. So a leader who speaks in visual terms to visual learners will build a relationship based on trust and understanding quite quickly, while asking them how they feel about something may be seen as quite irrelevant. Consequently, leaders need to learn to modify their language to suit the person speaking. This does not mean trying to work out what others are, but rather learning to operate on multiple channels. For example, if someone responds to the question 'What happened?' in terms of 'I saw...', the leader might add the further question, 'Were there other things which caught your eye?' Leaders need to become adept at changing language to suit the person contributing and also be aware of situations where participants need to be shown different modes of functioning. Genie Laborde gives many examples of the skills needed for this in *Influencing with integrity* (Palo Alto: Syntony Publishing, 1984).

Summary

In these first two chapters we have looked at the purpose of Christian leadership, and the ways Christian learners learn. How do all these ideas fit together? The following factors affect adult education in Bible study groups, and we will use them as a framework for summarising our thinking:

1. the nature of the learner;

2. the nature of the content;

3. the nature of the resources;

4. the context of learning;

5. the facilitator.[16]

These five elements must be effectively balanced in order to assist in learning.

1. The nature of the learner

We have highlighted that our leadership is to serve the learner. It must be learner focused. The Bible study group leader seeks to provide what the members (as learners) need for growth and development. To do this effectively, the leader must develop an understanding of what motivates adults to learn, and how to help them through the learning cycle in a way that takes account of their individual learning preferences.

2. The nature of the content

Distinctively Christian content is at the heart of Bible study group leadership. The primary purpose is to promote personal spiritual growth. This form of leadership seeks to provide people with knowledge which enables them to make sense of their world, encouraging them to grow in their relationship with God. This content needs to be delivered in a way that recognises the nature of the learner and the learning cycle. Leadership involves prompting individuals to consider the application and integration of the scriptural content, and also providing opportunities for individuals to critically reflect on their understanding and practice.

---

16. R. Wickett, *Models of adult religious education practice* (Birmingham: Religious Education Press, 1991), 35.

3. The nature of the resources

The resource base for learning in the Bible study group is both learner and teacher coming together to consider Scripture. The leader has technical skills and expertise which assist in the understanding of Scripture. Leaders also bring their own experience as learners and come with their personal outlooks which can provide a fresh perspective. However, the leader is only half of the resources. The members are also a resource. They have life experiences, insights, and particular needs which they bring to learning. They are able to read, analyse and consider Scripture and therefore are able to provide their own biblical input.

4. The context of learning

The context of learning actually shapes the learning. It was noted earlier that people come to learning seeking such things as ministry skills training, social change and personal growth. Adults each have a unique personal life context. They come to learning with needs, concerns, biases, weaknesses, strengths, and challenges. They also bring their current phase of life, the social context in which they live, and their personal histories. Bible study group leadership needs to recognise this personal life context, and assist people to learn within it, helping them to see connections, influences, opportunities and limitations brought about by the actual context of learning.

5. The facilitator

The individual facilitating the learning is crucial. He or she is not passive in the learning process but actively engaged and as a result can either help or hinder the progress of the learner. The Bible study group leader must know what to do, why to do it, and how to do it well.

At the beginning of this chapter we asked you to consider the following questions:

> What were your most memorable learning experiences?
>
> Who has helped you learn the most?
>
> What things help you to learn?
>
> What things keep you from learning?
>
> In what ways is your approach to learning different from those around you?

By now you will be more aware of your own learning style and the reasons behind the answers you gave. Your preferred method for acquiring information will have been clarified and you may have become more aware of the way in which you run a Bible study.

 Consider the following questions in the light of what you have read:

How can I encourage and sustain adults educationally?

What can I learn from my group members?

How do adults learn, and how can I help my group members to learn?

Have these people changed or grown closer to God as a result of this Bible study?

How would I know if they had changed or grown closer to God?

In the next chapter, you will discover how to use the things you have learned to construct Bible studies which appeal to people with different learning styles.

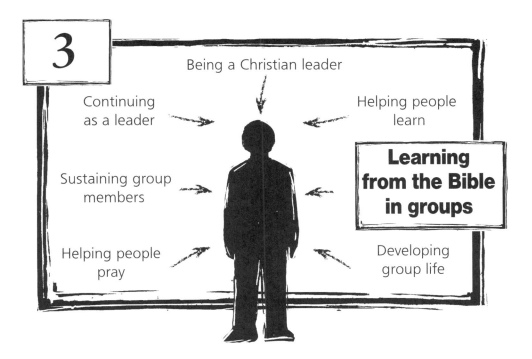

3

Being a Christian leader

Continuing as a leader

Helping people learn

Sustaining group members

Learning from the Bible in groups

Helping people pray

Developing group life

Using the Bible in groups is the very heart of a Bible study group, as it is primarily by studying the Bible that we grow as Christians. You must have skills in both handling the Bible, and in doing this in a group context. This chapter explores both these areas in depth.

We did not deal with this material first, even though we consider it the most important, because it builds on the material covered so far. Your commitment to studying the Bible in your group will arise out of your understanding of Christian leadership and your approach to leading the group will be shaped by your desire to help people learn.

The nature of Bible study

Effective Bible study is rather like detective work. One of our favourite mystery writers is P. D. James. She weaves intricate plots around her main character, Inspector Dalgiesh. He is very English, very proper, and always solves the crime.

If you were Inspector Dalgiesh, how would you solve this crime?

The corpse without hands lay in the bottom of a small sailing dinghy drifting within sight of the Suffolk coast. It was the body of a middle-aged man, a dapper little cadaver, its shroud a dark pin-striped suit which fitted the narrow body as elegantly in death as it had in life. The hand-made shoes still gleamed except for some scuffing of the toe caps, the silk tie was knotted under the prominent Adam's apple. He had dressed with careful orthodoxy for the town, this hapless voyager; not for this lonely sea; nor for this death.

It was early afternoon in mid-October and the glazed eyes were turned upwards to a sky of surprising blue across which the light south-west wind was dragging a few torn rags of cloud. The wooden shell, without mast or rowlocks, bounced gently on the surge of the North Sea so that the head shifted and rolled as if in restless sleep. It had been an unremarkable face even in life and death had given it nothing but a pitiful vacuity. The fair hair grew sparsely from a high bumpy forehead, the nose was so narrow that the white ridge of bone looked as if it were about to pierce the flesh; the mouth, small and thin-lipped, had dropped open to reveal two prominent front teeth which gave the whole face the supercilious look of a dead hare.[1]

The first step is to collect information. You would want to know who he was and how he died. Where have the tides and currents pushed the boat? Who would benefit from his death?

Next, interpret these observations to make sense of all the collected data. Form a theory about who are your most likely suspects, and check them against the information you have.

Once you have firm proof, the last stage would be to act upon the information by charging the murderer with the crime.

The process you followed is an 'inductive' process. First you observed and investigated: witnesses, clues, autopsy, interviews, and motives. Then you interpreted the information: suspects, alibis, and

---

1.   P.D. James, *Unnatural causes* (London: Sphere Books Ltd, 1967), 1.

theories. Finally you applied your interpretation: arrest, verdict, conviction.

'Induction' involves observing facts and then interpreting them to reach a conclusion, as shown in the following diagram.[2]

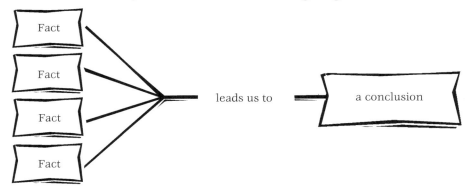

'Deduction', on the other hand, involves forming an idea about what might have happened, then looking for the facts to back up the theory, as shown below. If Inspector Dalgiesh had used a deductive approach, he would have identified a culprit and then set about proving the person's guilt. To do this, he would have collected only information that supported his case and then charged the assumed guilty party. This process is popularly known as framing someone.

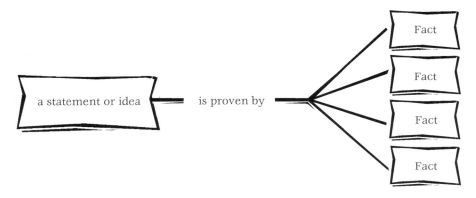

Our motor mechanic employs an inductive process when we take the car to him for repair, and our doctor treats us using the same approach. She observes the symptoms, interprets the information in her diagnosis and then decides what treatment to apply on the basis

---

2. This diagram and the next one were taken from unpublished notes by Dr Graeme Goldsworthy which identified the author as R. Yohn *Explore the Bible yourself.*

of this observation and interpretation. The process underlying effective Bible study is also inductive. It begins with observing the elements and specifics of the text, then interpreting them, and finally drawing conclusions which form the basis for the application of the Bible to our lives. This process is the foundation of personal Bible study and group study alike.

There are three basic steps in the process of moving towards understanding a text of the Bible: observation, interpretation and application. Remember that these are the steps of the learning cycle we examined in Chapter 2: 'Helping people learn'. These steps require you to find out what the text actually says before you try to determine its meaning and its application to your own life. An inductive approach begins with the text, a deductive approach begins with an idea and seeks to support it from Scripture. Deduction begins with generalisations and looks to the Bible to provide proof texts. By its very nature deduction tends to be slanted and subjective. Robert Traina says deduction 'produces those who dictate to the Scriptures, rather than those who listen to the Scriptures'.[3] Given that Scripture is God's revelation, such an approach is inappropriate.

On the other hand, induction seeks to be objective and impartial. It is difficult for us to be truly impartial, as the process of observation always occurs within our individual frame of meaning. Nevertheless, observation demands that you examine the particulars of the text and that your conclusions be based upon those particulars. Traina concludes that inductive study 'produces hearers rather than speakers and the nature of the Scriptures requires hearers'.[4]

The process of Bible study

Observation, interpretation and application are fundamental to effective Bible study. At the end of a Bible study, every member of your group should be confidently able to answer these three questions:

✦ What does the text actually say?

✦ What does the text mean?

✦ How do we respond to what the text means?

---

3. R. Traina, *Methodical Bible study* (Kentucky: Asbury Theological Seminary, 1952), 7.
4. Traina, 7.

We teach these three basic questions to our groups so that they know what we are doing as we work through a study. At the end of a study we ask the questions to check we have satisfactorily covered a passage. If anyone feels we have not adequately answered one of them we need to revisit it and deal with it in more detail. If the group has answered these questions, it means we have adequately covered the observation, interpretation and application process.

Exegesis and hermeneutics are technical words you might hear used with reference to Bible study. Exegesis simply means observing what is in the text while hermeneutics is the process of interpretation. We use observation and interpretation as they are easier to spell and make more sense to your average group member.

Bible study leadership requires you to develop the skills and techniques which help you answer the three basic questions.

If you find you are not familiar with the material in this section, we recommend you make it a priority to read the following:

Andrew Reid, *Postcard from Palestine,* 2nd ed. (Sydney: Matthias Media, 1997).

H. Hendricks and W. Hendricks, *Living by the Book* (Chicago: Moody, 1991).

Skills for observation – What does the text actually say?

Observation is obviously the vital component of any investigative work. Without good investigation Inspector Dalgiesh could arrest the wrong person or let the criminal go free. Without good observation, it is very easy to misinterpret or misapply the Bible.

The first step in Bible study is the step of producing a modern translation of the original languages. Thankfully this is done for us by scholars who exercise great skill and care. If you do not have a good modern translation we recommend you buy *The New International Version* or *The New Revised Standard Version,* or another produced by the International Bible Society.

So how do we do good investigation of the Bible? To establish what the text actually says, we need to look for eight elements.[5]

---

5. This section has been developed from ideas contained in Ada Lum, *Bringing the Bible to life* (Harrow: International Fellowship of Evangelical Students, 1987). This is an excellent video and workbook course explaining how to study the Bible.

1. The overall meaning of the text

We must develop a feel for the overall shape of the text by reading it in the context of what comes before and after it. The authors of the Bible did not intend paragraphs to be studied in isolation but wrote whole books for their readers. There is a saying that 'a text without a context is a pretext for a proof text'. Psalm 137:9 provides an example of how a verse taken out of context can be grossly misunderstood. The psalmist writes 'happy shall they be who take your little ones and dash them against the rock!' From the context, he clearly is not giving advice to baby sitters.

We should:

read the passage;

read the passage, in its context;

read the passage, in its context, in its book;

read the passage, in its context, in its book, in its biblical category;

read the passage, in its context, in its book, in its biblical category, in its Testament;

read the passage, in its context, in its book, in its biblical category, in its Testament, in the Bible.

This involves lots of reading, but it means that you are dealing with the Bible as a revelation which has a particular intended meaning by God for his people.

2. Specific facts and details

Once you understand the context, the next step is to work on the specific facts and details of the passage. This is where the comparison to Inspector Dalgiesh and his crime-solving prowess is most clearly seen. Ask seven simple questions to gather your facts:

✦ **Who?**
Who are the participants in the story or letter?

✦ **Where?**
Where are the events set?

✦ **When?**
When did the events take place? Examine the time/context/situation of the passage.

✦ **What?**
What is the focus or action of the text?

✦ **How?**
What is the method and manner of the argument or action?

✦ **Why?**

What is the reason, purpose or cause of the argument or action?

✦ **So?**

What is the result or climax of the text?

3. Grammatical structure

While many of us may have unpleasant memories of studying grammar at school, it is of great assistance when studying the Bible. The meaning of a passage is best understood when the language, grammar and syntax are carefully studied. The tense of verbs indicates whether something happens in the past, present or future. The use of commands, statements, descriptions and conditional clauses conveys sense and meaning within a passage.

4. How persuasion is used

The form of persuasion used helps us understand how important writers consider their message to be, and how they see one idea linking to another. If the writer is using exhortation rather than warning or command, then this will influence your interpretation of the passage. Writers might also use advice, promises and questions.[6]

5. How writers develop their thoughts

How are ideas or events related or developed in the passage? Writers can develop their thoughts by telling a story, building a theory or drawing a comparison. The things to look for include:

logical relationships;

cause and effect;

the means to an end;

general statements;

progression of ideas or actions;

comparisons and contrasts.[7]

The aim is to understand the progression of the argument through the passage. If the writer develops a logical argument then it is appropriate to try to determine the reasoning behind the logic and how the author put it together. If the author develops a plot, follow the story to see how it advances to its climax.

---

6.   Lum, 16.
7.   Lum, 17.

6. How things are emphasised

Where is the passage focused? How is this indicated? Different writers employ different techniques to inform the reader of the significance of their statements. Below are a few which are used in Scripture:

repetitions;

figures of speech;

proportions;

contrasts;

comparisons;

illustrations.[8]

For instance, the Gospel writers indicate the significance of Jesus' death by the amount of space dedicated to the last week of Jesus' life. In 1 Corinthians, Paul emphasises the difference between the gospel message and Judaism by contrasting a range of elements. In 1 and 2 Kings, the writer emphasises the failure of the monarchy by continually repeating that 'the King did what was evil in the sight of the Lord'.

Figures of speech require special attention. It is important to identify them (observation) so that they are not taken literally, and it is important to correctly grasp them (interpretation) so the full meaning of a passage can be understood.

Many passages of Scripture could generate some very strange doctrines if taken literally. Jesus said, 'I am the bread of life. Whoever comes to me will never be hungry, and whoever believes in me will never be thirsty' (John 6:35). This does not mean that we never feel hunger or thirst, nor does it mean we consume his physical body. Paul's comment in Galatians 5:12, 'I wish those who unsettle you would castrate themselves!', is not to be understood as a principle of church discipline! 'I bore you on eagles' wings and brought you to myself' (Exodus 19:4) is not a description of Israel's mode of travel during the Exodus!

7. How connectives are used

There is a silly but very useful little question: 'What is the therefore there for?' Linking words indicate progression in thought, or a

---

8.   Lum, 17.

change in direction. They help us to delve into the original intention of the authors as they wrote. The sort of words used to link ideas and develop an argument include:[9]

but	then	therefore
though	as	because
in order	so that	and
however	if … then	that
when	so	since
yet	while	for

In Romans, Paul begins an argument which progresses by the use of 'therefore', 'so that' and 'since'. Noticing these connectives will help you follow his argument.

8. The living document

Your imagination is also a useful tool when studying the Bible, if it is used wisely and doesn't add things which are not actually recorded. Scripture is not merely words on a page but a record of the way God has acted with people over history. They are real people in real situations with real reactions and emotions. Reconstructing the event or situation on the basis of the information in the text may help us to see the text as a living document.

For example, in a study on Philippians 1, it is normal to ask questions such as 'What does Paul say about evangelism in the passage?' Consider what happens when you ask people to determine from the passage 'How does Paul feel about evangelism?' The results, while both true to the text, are completely different. For instance, in answer to the first question the group might say that Paul says evangelism is really important and that he does not mind being in jail for it. The second question however could elicit the response that he is completely passionate and perhaps even a bit obsessed by it. The question which flows from this observation is, of course, 'Why? Why is Paul so passionate about evangelism?'

Part of using your imagination wisely is that you keep asking questions of the text. Often having asked and answered the opening observation questions, the leader and the group move on. But there

---

9. Lum, 19.

is much more to be discovered if you keep asking questions. Do not accept the easy answer and then move on. Imagine what can be learned by asking questions like:

'How is this idea related to that idea?'

'What is not said?'

'What else is involved in this?'

'How can this be true when...?'

'If this is so, could it be that...?'

Skills for interpretation – What does the text mean?

Let us return to Inspector Dalgiesh. Having observed all the facts, he then has to make some theories and construct hypotheses. He tries to develop an understanding of the crime that accommodates all the information gathered in the investigation. Likewise, Bible study involves trying to develop an understanding of the passage that accommodates all the information gathered during observation. Interpretation involves amassing all the details observed in the text and seeking to unite them into a coherent whole. It means making connections, asking why. This is the theorisation component of the learning cycle from Chapter 2.

At this stage we are still not talking about ourselves or our times, but are trying to understand the writer's intention for the original readers. We are seeking to interpret the meaning of the passage. One of the major difficulties in doing this is the gap between us and the original readers. This gap is a consequence of both language and culture, and a consequence of our living after the resurrection of Christ. The gap created by language and culture can be crossed by the use of reliable translations and reference materials, while the theological gap created by the death and resurrection of Christ is crossed by careful consideration of how a passage fits within the total story of Scripture.

The most significant danger in interpretation is the possibility of adding to the text information you imagine to be there. Under these conditions your understanding of the Bible is simply a product of your imagination. Consequently, it is critical to work hard at interpretation.

Interpreting Scripture requires humility and dependence on the

Spirit of God. Isaiah reminds his readers that 'my thoughts are not your thoughts, nor are your ways my ways, says the LORD' (Isaiah 55:8). At times we will be reminded that God is infinitely greater than us and we must accept him as he reveals himself to us. We are not the judge of Scripture, but it is the judge of us.

General principles for interpretation can be applied to every passage we study.

1. Bible categories

C. S. Lewis wrote 'the first qualification for judging any piece of workmanship from a corkscrew to a cathedral is to know what it is – what it was intended to do and how it is meant to be used'.[10] Likewise, the books of the Bible were written in different ways for different purposes. They belong to different categories, or 'genres'. Some are meant to be taken literally, while others use poetic imagery. A crucial question for biblical interpretation is: 'Are you taking the literary category of the passage into account?'

The Bible is made up of many different forms of literature. Andrew Reid calls the Bible 'the literary library of a nation'.[11] He comments 'we have usually been taught to read the Bible in only one gear, usually the one in which we read the epistles of Paul'. He says that if we are going to understand what the author wanted to say to the original hearers, we must learn to recognise the different types of literature in the Bible, and how to accurately interpret them.[12]

You do not read a parking ticket in the same way you read a love letter, and you do not read a classified advertisement the same way you read the editorial. The main categories of biblical literature, and examples in each category, include:

Apocalyptic *(Revelation)*	Gospel *(Mark)*
Law *(Leviticus)*	Parable *(2 Samuel 12)*
Prophecy *(Isaiah)*	Sermon *(Hebrews)*
Epistle *(Romans)*	History *(1 and 2 Kings)*
Narrative *(Ruth)*	Poetry *(Job)*
Prayer *(Psalms)*	Wisdom *(Ecclesiastes)*

---

10. C. S. Lewis, *A preface to paradise lost* (London: Oxford University Press, 1942), 1.
11. A. Reid, *Postcard from Palestine* (Sydney: St Matthias Press, 1989), 43.
12. Reid, 43.

Each of these needs to be treated differently if you are to deal with the Bible intelligently. If you read a passage of poetry, you would not expect to be able to answer questions of history and architecture from it. No, poetry is emotive and its form is often repetitive. The category or genre of the text is one of the first keys for correctly interpreting a passage.

These features help us recognise each category and guide our interpretation:

- ✦ **Apocalyptic**
  Images of God, judgment, hope, and spiritual reality.

- ✦ **Epistle**
  Arguments and relationships.

- ✦ **Gospel**
  Identity, priorities, death and resurrection of Jesus.

- ✦ **History**
  Origin and progression of God's people.

- ✦ **Law**
  Requirements for living in relation to God, in certain periods.

- ✦ **Narrative**
  Plot and characterisation.

- ✦ **Parable**
  Metaphor and simile.

- ✦ **Poetry**
  Emotional response, and the object that evoked the emotion.

- ✦ **Prophecy**
  What God intends to do and why.

- ✦ **Prayer**
  God's people communicating with him.

- ✦ **Sermon**
  Proving, explaining or exhorting.

- ✦ **Wisdom**
  How to live well in the world.

There are numerous books written on the different forms of literature in the Bible. We recommend you add at least one of these to your reference library:

Andrew Reid, *Postcard from Palestine,* 2nd ed. (Sydney: Matthias Media, 1997).

Douglas Stuart and Gordon Fee, *How to read the Bible for all it's worth* (Michigan: Zondervan, 1982).

2. Harmony in Scripture

The second principle for interpreting the Bible is harmony in Scripture. It is a simple concept. If we believe that God inspired the Bible then we can rely on a harmonious message throughout.

Scripture is God's deliberate revelation of himself. God does not contradict himself, and his revelation is not disjointed and random. Consequently, each passage should be interpreted with a view to the whole Bible and so that it makes sense in the context of the whole. Do not interpret one text in such a way that it contradicts others in the Bible. Rather, we must work hard to integrate our understanding of Scripture into one total package. We should exercise great care when a whole doctrine is built on one or two verses, and we should understand hard texts in the light of information from plain texts. Apparent paradoxes such as the fact that Jesus is both divine and human need to be carefully worked through. Some ideas are difficult to understand, but this is not surprising when you remember that humans are trying to understand God. At times, passages may appear to be irreconcilable, and we need humility and patience as we wait upon God to give understanding.

One simple technique for interpreting short difficult sections is Question Reduction. Begin by listing all the possible meanings of the verses, including those meanings which are patently wrong. Then, using the context of the passage (the surrounding verses and chapters) eliminate those interpretations which are inconsistent with the rest of the text. Finally, use cross references (especially from the same author) and commentaries, to decide on which explanation best suits the passage as a whole. Consider what the text would mean with each different answer, and which meaning is most consistent with the book and leads to the greatest harmony in Scripture.

3. Biblical theology

The third principle for interpretation is closely related to the second. We need to develop an understanding of the overall story of the Bible. Biblical theology is the lens through which we interpret Scripture. Graeme Goldsworthy writes 'Biblical theology gives us a means of dealing with problem passages in the Bible by relating them to the one message of the Bible'.[13] Linking a passage into the overall story of the Bible enables us to see the context of a passage and how the meaning of the whole of Scripture is being developed in each particular portion.

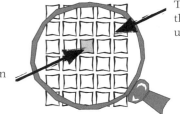

The whole acts as a lens through which we understand the part

The part is understood in relation to the whole

As a Bible study group leader you need to develop a biblical theology which helps you interpret Scripture. The following books provide helpful introductions:

> Graeme Goldsworthy, *According to plan* (Leicester: IVP, 1991).

> Mark Strom, *Days are coming* (Sydney: Hodder and Stoughton, 1989).

4. Salvation history

The fourth principle for interpretation is to recognise where a passage fits into the history of God's salvation of humanity. Salvation history, or redemptive history, is a term often used in connection with biblical theology. It describes the entire account of God's dealing with humanity. It begins with creation in Genesis and runs through Scripture to the new creation in Revelation. God has been deliberately working in history to bring his purposes to fulfilment in Christ. Within this history, God's covenant with his people can be seen as a

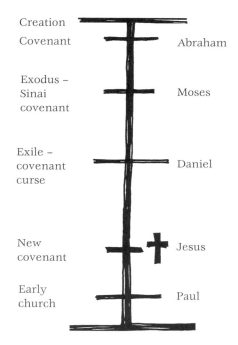

Creation

Covenant — Abraham

Exodus – Sinai covenant — Moses

Exile – covenant curse — Daniel

New covenant — Jesus

Early church — Paul

---

13.   G. Goldsworthy, *According to plan* (Leicester: IVP, 1991), 24.

unifying theme throughout Scripture. Bill Dumbrell writes, 'The Old Testament as a whole is a record of how Israel's thinking advanced from creation to covenant at Sinai to a new covenant calculated to lead to a new creation ... we must be aware of this theological progression and the reasons for it as we read the literature'.[14]

When studying an Old Testament passage, we always get the group to consider the place of the passage in relation to the progress of the covenant. The prophets are a simple example. Those writing prior to the Babylonian Exile emphasise the need to remember the covenant and be faithful to God, while prophets during the exile focus on God's faithfulness to his covenant in spite of circumstances.

It can be helpful to draw a time line like the one on the previous page, and have the group place the significant characters and events upon it to establish the context of the passage we are studying. This context will help you find the emphasis within a passage.

5. The grace of God

Grace is an incredibly simple doctrine. It means undeserved blessing freely bestowed on humanity by God.[15] Philip Hughes writes that it is 'a concept which is at the heart not only of Christian theology, but also of all genuinely Christian experience'.[16] God's grace means he chooses to love us before, and independently of, anything we do in response to him. Grace means we were reconciled to God while we were enemies, made alive while we were dead, justified while we were sinners.

This is an essential doctrine in interpretation as it means we must avoid any interpretation of Scripture that shifts the focus away from what God has done for us and onto what we do for him.

6. The character of God and the fulfilment of Scripture in Christ

It is important for us to study the Old Testament, although many groups practically ignore it. People are anxious about interpreting Old Testament passages correctly. This is a real concern, but it is not insurmountable. It is often said that in Sunday School the correct answer to any question is 'Jesus' or 'God'. While this is an exaggeration, it is a useful reminder that pivotal to interpreting the Bible is the centrality of Christ and the character of God.

---

14. W. Dumbrell, *The faith of Israel* (Leicester: Apollos, 1988), 10.
15. P. Hughes, 'Grace' in W. Elwell, *Dictionary of evangelical theology* (Grand Rapids: Baker, 1984), 479.
16. Hughes, 'Grace', 479.

The Old Testament is the history of God's dealings with humanity, which reaches its climax with Jesus. We now have a full explanation of things which are only partially revealed in the Old Testament. When studying the Old Testament, we need to read each passage as recorded in its own right, but also in the light of God's complete revelation. By studying it we develop an understanding of God's character: his holiness, sovereignty, righteousness, love, judgment, mercy and jealousy. We also gain an understanding of God's covenant and his dealings with his people. We have examples of prayer, praise and worship which we can imitate. We find examples of faith and obedience to challenge us. We find passages which give wisdom on how to live well in God's world, and others which provide a graphic reminder of spiritual realities we often forget.

When studying Old Testament passages, we consider:

> what the passage means in its own context;

> how the passage contributes to our understanding of the New Testament; and

> how the Cross influences our understanding of the passage.

In the Old Testament we find explanations of such concepts as redemption, atonement, sacrifice and faithfulness, which we need to understand in order to fully comprehend the Cross and the New Testament era. The death and resurrection of Jesus was the turning point in history, inaugurating a new age and reconciling people to God. Graeme Goldsworthy summarises the relationship of the Old Testament to Christ in this diagram which emphasises the Old Testament's fulfilment in Christ.[17]

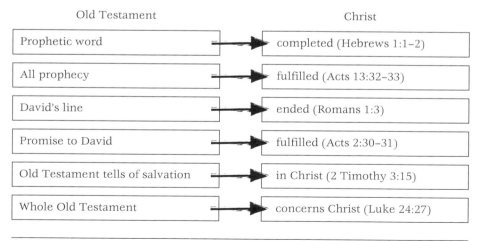

Old Testament	Christ
Prophetic word	completed (Hebrews 1:1–2)
All prophecy	fulfilled (Acts 13:32–33)
David's line	ended (Romans 1:3)
Promise to David	fulfilled (Acts 2:30–31)
Old Testament tells of salvation	in Christ (2 Timothy 3:15)
Whole Old Testament	concerns Christ (Luke 24:27)

---

17. Goldsworthy, 63.

This works two ways: the Old Testament points forward to Jesus and his death; and Jesus is the lens which brings major parts of the Old Testament into focus.

Old Testament points to the Cross

We look back to the Old Testament through the Cross

 and

We find it helpful to think of the Cross as a lens, because it emphasises that some details are radically changed when seen through the lens, while other details remain unaltered.

Two books which we have found really helpful in approaching the Old Testament are:

> William J. Dumbrell, *Faith of Israel* (Leicester: Apollos, 1989).
>
> Graeme Goldsworthy, *Gospel and Kingdom* (Exeter: Paternoster, 1981).

7. The overlap of the ages

The final concept which guides interpretation is the fact that we live in the overlap of two ages: the present evil age, and the age to come when all evil will be swept away. The age to come was inaugurated by the resurrection of Christ and we already participate in it through our union with Christ, but it will not be fully realised until the return of Christ and his judgment of all things.

The believer now lives in this overlap of the ages.

We live between the Cross and the return of Christ.

We are still part of the present age, but we are also already participating in the age to come. Knowing what is going to happen changes how you view the future. An example of this sort of tension is the period of time between receiving your exam results and actually graduating. We are united with Christ and we have the Holy

Spirit. We currently wait for the culmination of what we already have. This creates a tension between the 'now' and the 'not yet' which we must strive to maintain when interpreting passages.

Resources for interpretation

Interpretation is an area where good commentaries and Bible dictionaries are of great assistance. However, not all commentaries and resources are written with a commitment to the Bible as the Word of God and to Christ as his risen Son. A useful guide when deciding what is worth using is to refer to a commentary survey such as the one found in *How to read the Bible for all it's worth* by Stuart and Fee (Michigan: Zondervan, 1982).

We suggest you consider getting the *New Bible Dictionary* and possibly some commentaries from the 'Tyndale' Commentary Series or the 'Bible Speaks Today' Series. These are all published by Inter-Varsity Press and are written with a commitment to biblical truth and personal faith in Jesus. We have also found the 'Reading the Bible today' series (edited by Dr Paul Barnett and published by Aquila Press) to be of great assistance and value. Our goal has been to acquire a good commentary on every book of the Bible. While few of us can afford to do this at one time, we have managed to do it over a number of years.

Skills for application –
How do we respond to what the text means?

The final stage of the process is to apply what we have learned to our lives. This is where Inspector Dalgiesh would act on his conclusions and arrest the culprit. Application is important to Bible study because the Bible is God's word. We study it in order to hear God speak to us, so we might know and love him, and live as his people. Application is not the additional step at the end of Bible study for those who are really keen, but the culmination of all that precedes it. We study the Bible in order to apply it to ourselves. To fail to do this is to miss the whole point of studying the Bible.

Many people suggest you ask these simple questions of each passage:

> Is there a command for me to obey?

Is there a reason for thanksgiving, worship or praise?

What does this passage teach me about God?

What does this passage teach me about Jesus?

How does this passage fit with what I already know?

Is there a promise to claim?

Is there an example to follow?

Is there a sin to avoid or confess?

What does this passage teach me about myself?

What does this passage teach me about others?

While these are helpful in identifying issues raised by a passage, they are preliminary questions. The really important question is simply:

✦ What will you do in response to this passage?

This is the heart of application – acting differently in response to God's word. We should always expect Scripture to be demanding change as we move closer to Christ and become more like him.

Application should involve concrete behaviours. In order to help people be concrete, we often ask them to describe, write down or tell another, one or two specific achievable things they will do as a result of this passage. We prefer using 'will' to 'should', as we want people to move from ideas to action when discussing application. After the What will you do? question, we encourage a group to discuss:

✦ How and when will you do it?

✦ What will help you do it?

✦ What will hinder you?

While Scripture has a specific meaning which we need to work hard at finding, this does not mean that the application will be identical for each person in a group. Rather, each of us has to work through what it means for us to respond appropriately within our own context. Rod's sister Kerrie, who has three small children at school and works from home, will be faced with quite different issues and struggles to his father John, who runs a dairy farm and whose children have grown and left home. Kerrie and John will respond differently to a passage, even though they agree on its meaning.

The application of Bible study has both vertical and horizontal dimensions – focused on God and on other people. Jesus said the great commandment is 'you shall love the Lord your God with all your heart, with all your soul, with all your mind and with all your strength. The second is this "you shall love your neighbour as yourself" ' (Mark 12:30–31a). The goal of Bible study is to grow in our relationship with God the Father, with our Lord Jesus Christ and with those around us. As the Bible should be shaping every part of our lives, it is helpful to encourage people to examine the application of a passage to the big areas of life such as:

worship	personal spiritual life
relationships	work
family	recreation
church	money

In a group setting, take the risk and be more honest, personal and specific when discussing the application of a text. For example, it is better to say 'I find that hard because...' rather than 'Don't you think that would be hard?' This enables the group to move beyond the superficial to wrestle with a passage. If you are courageous in trusting others, you may find they follow suit.

The quality of our observation and interpretation is crucial in laying the groundwork for application. Knowing the purpose of a passage enables us to apply it correctly. Whenever our situation corresponds exactly to that faced by the original readers, God's word to us is the same as it was to them. However, this happens rarely, so we need to identify the underlying principles. We can then apply those principles to our situation today. Ask: 'What would the original writer write to us?'

It is important to remember that we do not need an application for every detail in a passage. Rather, we should concentrate on responding to the main thrust of the passage. We once heard it suggested that Jesus resting on a pillow at the back of the boat during the storm in Mark 4:38 was an example of Jesus 'resting in God's protection', and the application was that we too should 'rest in God's protection'. While it is true that we should rely on God, this is not the point of this passage. Instead, the focus of the passage is Mark 4:41 where the disciples ask 'Who then is this, that even the wind and the sea obey him?' The passage is part of Mark's exploration of Jesus' identity. As a consequence, the application should involve how we respond to Jesus.

Finally, we must remember the harmony in Scripture principle. The applications derived from a passage should always be consistent with what we know the Bible teaches elsewhere. We occasionally hear people using passages like 'Above all, maintain constant love for one another, for love covers a multitude of sins' (1 Peter 4:8) in order to justify sexually immoral behaviour, even though other passages clearly rebuke those who engage in it. You cannot use one passage of the Bible to validate sinful behaviour when other passages clearly condemn it.

Actually preparing and running a group Bible study

We have now covered the principles behind the three steps to effective Bible study:

✦   Observation – What does the text actually say?

✦   Interpretation – What does the text mean?

✦   Application – How do we respond to what the text means?

How will you help your group answer these questions? There are four phases involved, each taking place within the context of prayerful dependence on God.

Phase 1: Understand the passage for yourself

Read the passage numerous times; ask hard questions; find out which bits you do not understand. It is useful to copy the text onto an A4 page so that you can scribble all over it, draw connecting lines, circle hard ideas or repeated words. Look for all the things explained in 'Skills for observation'.

When you have done this, read other material if you need to. What do some commentaries say about this passage? Does the Bible dictionary help with any customs, traditions, or other background details? Find out more about the people, the place, the time, or the situation. How is their situation different to or the same as ours?

This is the beginning of the interpretation phase. Think about why the writer might write this. What principles are behind the words? Did the writer have something particular in mind for the original readers to understand? What difference does living after Jesus' resurrection and ascension make to our understanding?

Then it is time to think about how the passage applies to you. How do the principles apply to your life? What changes do you need to make? What corrections to your beliefs are needed and what difference will that change in belief make in your life?

It is important to go through the whole observation, interpretation, application phase for ourselves before we even begin to think about applying it to others. Bible study is not merely an academic process but rather the process of changing the lives of God's people, your own included. This will also give you a strong grounding when you come to work through it with other people.

This is the first stage in preparation. By the end of it, you should be able to confidently answer the three basic questions: you will know what the text actually says; you will have considered what it means; and you will have applied it to yourself.

Phase 2: Develop a process

The second stage in preparation is working out how to assist the group through the observation, interpretation, application process for themselves. The way many people run Bible studies indicates that they see no need for this. They approach the study as if the next step is simply: 'Tell people'. That is a sermon, not a Bible study.

This second step involves thinking about how to help people learn. As we discussed in the previous chapter, people learn in different ways. We also saw that adults learn best when they learn for themselves. It is frequently assumed that the leader asks questions and the group answers them. This can be boring and often results in the group playing 'guess what the leader thinks' as they go through the study. Adults need to be able to 'get their hands dirty' in the passage. Many people say they learned the most when they had to prepare to lead the Bible study. It makes sense, then, for the members of your Bible study group to experience the same thrill of working on a passage and gaining the meaning from it for themselves. Your job is to lead them on a safari into the text.

This means relying less on the traditional question and answer approach, and developing other creative activities which get people working on the passage. Given that adults learn best when they are engaged in the activity and having their own questions answered, we need a method which causes the group to ask questions about the text. Usually group members will ask the same questions the leader would have asked. Remember that the fundamental difference between this and traditional question/answer studies is that when group members ask the questions they want to know the answers.

This is a major shift in thinking for many people. Therefore we need to learn methods for helping the group do observation and interpretation. The next section contains numerous possibilities for observation activities with sample Bible studies attached. Work on the list for yourself and develop new ideas that you can use with your group. Application flows more easily if the foundation work is done well.

The passage to be studied will influence the method used in studying it. As the Bible contains a variety of genres, it is unrealistic to expect every activity to be appropriate for every passage. This links back to our discussion of Bible categories and how each category has one or two keys which help us understand it. Look hard at the passage and try to determine the writer's framework for the text: logical argument, imagery, metaphor, comparison, contrast.

> **When group members ask the questions they want to know the answers.**

As leader, you need to take into account such factors in determining the best method for approaching the passage the group is working on. We usually find there are a couple of approaches available for any particular passage and we choose one that adds variety for the group. Our rule is to limit our use of an approach to once every six weeks. This avoids repetition and helps ensure we cater to the range of learning styles within the group.

In addition, consider the type of interpretation questions which might arise from doing the observation activity, and how you might use these to move the group towards understanding the text. Also identify any additional information which the group will need to interpret the passage adequately.

Phase 3: Trial run

The third step in preparation is giving it a trial run. Having worked out an observation activity which is appropriate to the passage, complete it yourself as preparation. This way you know it actually works. Over time you may develop a good sense of what works and what doesn't, but we still find that some great ideas don't actually work well in practice and other apparently lacklustre ideas work incredibly well in practice. Creativity, experimentation, practice and perseverance are the keys to developing good techniques over time.

Having completed the observation activity, record any further interpretation questions which result from your own research. Combined with the questions you have previously developed, and the ones which arise during the study, these will enhance the in-depth discussion.

Phase 4: Running the study

Launch straight into the study, with the group reading the passage and then working on it for themselves. As an aside, we do not recommend you develop the practice of having an introductory question in the study. This pre-empts the study and tells people what to think about the passage before they read it.

The first goal is for the group to know what the passage actually says. Many of the activities outlined below involve the group researching and reporting back. Once they have collected the information, ask for questions or comments about the passage. Once again, the object is to get the group doing the work. If the leader asks the questions, the group might be interested in the answers, but if observation of the passage has raised issues and dilemmas, the group will ask the questions and they will want to know the answers. This moves the group into interpretation – working out what the passage actually means.

If the group has worked hard on the passage, the interpretation phase is not so difficult. The obvious questions are: Why did the writer record this? What were the principles behind the specific examples given?

Asking people to make connections and work out the purpose in writing is the background work to understanding how this passage applies to us today. The final stage then is application, working out how we respond to what Scripture teaches. The group members need to consider what the writer might have written to them, how the principles apply and what difference it will make in their lives. The better the work done in the observation and interpretation phases, the easier it is to apply the passage at the end.

Methods for doing observation with a group

This section provides a range of observation activities which enable

the group to engage with the text, encouraging them to ask questions. Each method includes an example based on that method, indicated by the symbol at left, in order to demonstrate its use. Note how the example for each observation technique adds suggestions for interpretation and application.

Most of the methods we use for observation involve the use of paper and pens. We usually write on butcher's paper to help people in the group interact, or make a copy of the text for underlining and circling ideas and words. Most people find it easier to keep track of a discussion when they can see the information clearly before them, and working with paper and pens gives the activists in the group something to do. We also find that people are reluctant to write in Bibles which may have been quite expensive, so having a copy of the text allows people to underline and circle without reservation.

Good quality, thick felt pens are vital if you hope for others to be able to see what people have written or produced, and we recommend you acquire three or four dozen felt pens which can be used by your group.

 Choose two or three passages from the Bible, each representing a different genre or literary category. As you read the following descriptions, consider which observation techniques would work best with the passages you have chosen.

1. SUMMARISE

This method is useful for long passages, especially narratives, because you can divide up the passage and have pairs allocated to each section. It is also good for passages which have clear ideas within each subsection. Summarising involves group members reading the passage and then presenting a summarised version to the rest of the group.

Divide the passage among the group. Ask each subgroup to carefully summarise their verses and report their findings. Encourage members to ask questions of those reporting back. We have found it best to have people work in pairs since this promotes discussion and sometimes even disagreement. It also enables the group to cover large passages quickly, and encourages everyone in the group to interact with the text.

Beware of using this method on a passage that is very familiar to the group. It won't engage their brains at all. It is better to use a different method.

Summarising works best with a large section of text when the passage leads to a conclusion or climax. The aim is to capture the key details leading up to the conclusion. This would work well for studying Exodus 15, the 'Song of Moses', which is a response to all God has done for his people Israel. Ask the group to examine chapters one to fourteen of Exodus in order to see how Exodus 15 is an appropriate response to the various acts of God.

Another passage where this technique could be used is Peter's statement in Mark 8:29 that Jesus is the Christ. In the middle of a series on Mark, or as an introduction to a series on the second half of Mark, you could ask the group to look over the eight previous chapters and summarise the reasons why Peter came to this conclusion. Having gathered the data for Peter's confession, the group members then consider the validity of his conclusion and whether they personally agree with it. We have actually had someone become a Christian when doing this particular study.

EXAMPLE: Daniel 9[18]

Observation

Read Daniel 9. Allocate the passage around the group and have each person or pair summarise these verses from Daniel 9: verses 4–6; verses 7–11; verses 12–14; verses 15–16; verses 17–19. Look for the essence of what is being communicated. The summary need not be recorded.

Are there questions or comments which arise from this exercise?

List the different parts of Daniel's prayer (for example, asking).

Interpretation

Consider the following questions:

What do we learn about the nature of Daniel's relationship with God?

What does the prayer and its response tell us about God?

Why is this prayer recorded in the Bible?

What does it tell us about praying as a community?

---

18. This study has been published in a fuller form by Karen Morris and Andrew Reid in *Kingdom of Dreams* (Sydney: St Matthias Press, 1997).

Application

Write a prayer for yourself using Daniel 9 as a guideline. Pray it.

(Other prayers which you could summarise and then pray for yourself include 1 Kings 8:23–53 and Matthew 6:9–13.)

---

2. PARAPHRASE

This technique is particularly useful for those passages which are very familiar but not always understood. We often find that people know the jargon of a passage but do not really understand the meaning of it. The aim of paraphrasing is for the group to translate a passage out of 'Bible English' into 'normal everyday English'.

Whole verses are often too long for one person to paraphrase easily, so we generally ask individuals to paraphrase a single phrase from each verse. It moves more quickly this way. After an individual's initial attempt at paraphrasing, we enlist the help of the rest of the group to fine-tune the first attempt. Doing this for every person takes the pressure off someone who is uncertain. Another way to relieve the tension is to have people work in pairs.

Newer Christians can feel intimidated because of their lack of Bible knowledge. Therefore you must constantly emphasise in the observation phase that the group is focusing on the passage at hand, not on all the extraneous information they can drag in.

The leader must work hard to ensure the theological content of a passage is maintained. For instance, while 'eldest child' may capture some of what it means to be the 'firstborn', it does not capture the sense of inheritance implicit in the biblical use of the word. The firstborn is the one who will inherit everything from the father, and may be better paraphrased as the 'heir'. It is crucial that the leader has worked on the passage in advance so nothing theologically significant is lost in the translation.

 ### EXAMPLE: Colossians 1:15–23

This passage is very dense and needs a fair amount of work before it becomes clear. The aim is for each person to be able to express it and relate it to him/herself. It would be helpful for the leader to have read a commentary on this passage.

Observation

Explain to the group that they are going to paraphrase the passage phrase by phrase. For example, Anne takes verse 15 and says 'Jesus

71

looks like God'. Then the whole group offers ideas which also come from the phrase, such as 'Jesus is the one who shows us what God is like'. Having formed a short translation we then move on to the next phrase. This way the group works through the passage in depth without publicly embarrassing anyone.

After every few verses recap the whole thing. Discuss any problems that people may have. If there is time, work to the end of the passage or complete it next week.

Interpretation

Ask: What is the main thrust of this passage? Why is Paul telling the Colossians these things?

Have someone read out Colossians 2:4. Ask: What 'plausible arguments' might Paul be arguing against in 1:15–23? What equivalent heresies are present today?

Application

Discuss how you respond to this description of Jesus.

Why is it important for us to have a theologically correct understanding of Jesus? What should we do to guard against heresy?

Pray.

3. COMPARE

Compare is a straightforward technique which requires the group to compare different passages by the same author, or passages by different authors on similar themes. Group members look for similarities and differences, changes in focus and underlying priorities in various passages. A good use of this technique is to ask the group to compare the introductions to Paul's letters and his prayers. Each of the epistles has an opening which is both similar and different to the other epistles. These can be compared in order to understand Paul more, or as an introduction to a particular letter. The exercise would raise the issues of who the intended recipients were, Paul's relationship with them, Paul's purpose in writing, and indicate possible themes which might be developed in the letter.

EXAMPLE: the Servant Songs in Isaiah 40–55[19]

To understand the Servant Songs, you must understand their context and the people to whom they were written.

Observation

Prior to reading the Servant Songs it is necessary to look at a passage that summarises the context. Read Isaiah 24:1–6 as a group.

The Old Testament talks about a Day of Judgment God has in store, and this is what Isaiah 24:1–6 addresses. What does this passage say will happen on that day and why? This is the context for Isaiah 40–55.

There are a number of key passages in the Servant Songs that address the issues raised in chapters 1–39. Read the passages, and then record the contrasts and similarities.

Passage	Contrasts	Similarities
Isaiah 42:1–4		
Isaiah 49:1–6		
Isaiah 50:4–9		
Isaiah 52:13–53:12		

Interpretation

Record the principle issues raised by these passages and consider how they connect with the issues raised in Isaiah 24:1–6.

Discuss how our knowledge of Jesus' death and resurrection affects our understanding of these passages.

Application

Discuss what difference these ideas make to you as individuals.

Pray.

4. NOTE

In its most basic form, noting involves underlining and circling. It requires a detail within the text which is emphasised or explained in some way. This can be a single word which is repeated, or it can be a theme which is developed from different angles in the passage. An

---

19. This study has been published in a fuller form by Karen Morris and Andrew Reid in *Two Cities* (Sydney: St Matthias Press, 1993).

example is Paul's use of 'I' statements in Romans 1:8–17. A simple study could have participants note all the 'I' statements Paul makes in this passage ('I thank...', 'I serve...', 'I remember...') by underlining them. They then consider the other uses of 'I' statements in Romans. This will highlight Paul's extensive use of them in this passage and their limited use elsewhere, and should cause people to ask 'Why?' As with most of these observation activities, this involves people working on the passage in the hope that they will be puzzled by something or notice something which makes them want to ask questions about the passage and its content. Noting simply involves the participants marking down particular ideas or words which generate questions in their minds.

EXAMPLE: Colossians 1:24–2:5

Observation

Read Colossians 1:24–2:5. Ask the group to note everything they can about the message that Paul presents in this passage (its nature, its content, its purpose, its effects). List these on butcher's paper, taking care to avoid any jargon.

Discuss any difficulties (mystery? present everyone perfect? what is lacking in Christ's afflictions?).

Interpretation

What is the central idea of the passage?

Why does Paul tell the Colossians this? What difference does it make if the Colossians know this?

Application

What difference does it make if we know this? What will you do in response to God's word?

Pray.

5. ORGANISE

This requires the participants to organise the ideas or themes of a passage into groups. Use this method on passages where there are distinct classifications which can be identified and explored. In Colossians 3:1-17, for example, the two groupings are things you put on and things you put off. Observing these two categories will help the group understand the distinction Paul is making between what we were and what we now are as Christians. The interpretation step involves discussing the significance of the grouping.

EXAMPLE: 2 Corinthians 2:14–5:10

See the example given for the next method, which uses organising to form two lists which are then contrasted. It is sometimes helpful to combine two easy activities in order to help a group fully explore a passage.

6. CONTRAST

This technique involves the group looking at the specifics of the passage and researching it carefully in order to identify contrasts contained within it. The process requires work from individuals so each person discovers the details of the passage and its meaning.

We have used this technique with Daniel 5, where the hand writes on the wall and Daniel is called to interpret it. We asked the group to draw up a table and to contrast Daniel vs Astrologers; Belshazzar vs Nebuchadnezzar; and the Real God vs Fake Gods. This activity clearly delineates the difference between belief and paganism.

EXAMPLE: 2 Corinthians 2:14–5:10

Observation

Read 2 Corinthians 2:14–5:10. This passage is a series of dichotomies or contrasts. To help you read the passage, complete the following table, picking out the contrasts presented by Paul. Do this step quickly so you have time for the rest of the study. At the bottom of the page have a space for the questions which arise in your mind as you go through the passage.

Negatives	Positives
To those who are perishing we are the smell of death	To those who are saved we are the fragrance of life.

Discuss any questions which come out of your careful reading of the passage. This is an important part of the study, so do not skip over it.

Have individuals describe their reactions to each of the columns.

Interpretation

Summarise the main point being made in each column.

Why do you think Paul wrote this section of the letter? What was his purpose or purposes?

Paul works from a number of background principles to develop the specific things he tells the Corinthians. From the text, what do you think these principles might have been?

Application

How do these principles apply to you personally? Read the positive column using it to describe yourself. What sort of reaction do you have?

Pray about these things.

7. IDENTIFY

When there are multiple groups interacting in a passage, considering each of them is helpful. Identify the separate groups and observe their actions and reactions. This is best for narrative where the author is developing plot and characterisations. It particularly helps clarify passages where the interactions are complicated. An example is John 4, where Jesus meets a Samaritan woman at a well. The characters include Jesus, the woman, the disciples and the townspeople. The task of dividing up the characters involved and working out their reactions, and then considering why they react the way they do, helps the group to work through the issues.

EXAMPLE: Mark 5:1-20

Observation

Read Mark 5:1–20. Ask participants to identify the people present at the scene of this event, what they did and their reason for what they did. Filling in this simple table will help clarify the action.

Participants	Action/reaction	Reason
Jesus		
The demon-possessed man		
Those tending the pigs		
The townspeople		
The disciples		

Interpretation

As Mark's Gospel is narrative, consider how this story contributes to the development of plot and characterisation. Discuss why Mark has included this story in his Gospel.

Discuss how this episode contributes to our understanding of Jesus.

Consider which group's response is most appropriate.

Application

Discuss how you respond to this story and what difference it makes to your understanding of Jesus.

Pray.

8. DRAWING

This is a technique we use only occasionally in Bible studies, but in the right place it can be very helpful and quite fun. When discussing biblical categories, we mentioned that apocalyptic passages in the Bible, such as Revelation and parts of Isaiah, use very rich imagery. They use graphic descriptions and vivid images which provoke reactions of fear, awe and wonder. This technique helps the group make sense of these passages. In particular, realising a description cannot be easily drawn helps a group recognise the description might be intended metaphorically rather than literally. On the other hand, a description in a narrative passage like that of Noah's ark can easily be drawn, and this may indicate the passage is to be understood literally.

When getting a group to draw you need to be adequately prepared with sheets of paper and good quality felt pens. Many people are afraid they will be made a fool of when it comes to drawing. It helps if you can honestly say 'I can't draw', or 'If you draw something recognisable then it obviously doesn't come from John's vision'. Emphasise that the aim is to observe what is said in the passage, not to produce an artistic treasure. Make it light-hearted and it will be much less stressful for everyone.

EXAMPLE: Daniel 7[20]

Observation

Read Daniel 7 and then draw the vision. Ask everyone to show the group their drawings, asking them to identify the key elements.

Ask the group to:

describe in their own words the feelings communicated about the beasts;

describe in their own words the feelings communicated about God;

describe the Kingdom of God;

describe Daniel's reaction to the vision.

Interpretation

What was the situation of the Jewish people when Daniel saw the vision? Refer to Psalm 137. What difference would the vision make to the Jewish people of Daniel's time?

What was the purpose of recording Daniel's vision?

What is the key verse in the passage? Why?

Application

Imagine a situation in which you think you would be completely overwhelmed. What does this passage tell you about such situations? What does the passage encourage us to keep believing in such circumstances?

Pray.

9. INTERVIEW

This technique is great fun. We have used it often to generate debate and discussion among the group. This has forced the group to really read the passage. The interview process has two forms.

In the first form, the leader formulates a series of journalistic interview questions to be asked of the characters in the passage. These are then distributed to the group and they pair up and

---

20. This study has been published in a fuller form by Karen Morris and Andrew Reid in *Kingdom of Dreams* (Sydney: St Matthias Press, 1997).

interview each other as if one was the journalist and the other the characters involved. The journalist is to act like a journalist – questioning further, probing, seeking explanations. After each question they swap roles. When the pairs have completed the questions, they record any they could not answer adequately, and bring these back for the whole group to discuss. Sample questions on Paul's epistle to Philemon might include:

Asked of Paul: What is your relationship with Philemon?

Asked of Onesimus: What has been the effect of Paul on you?

Asked of Paul: How do you feel about sending Onesimus back to Philemon?

Asked of Paul: Why are you sending Onesimus back to Philemon?

Asked of Onesimus: Why are you going back to Philemon?

Asked of Philemon: Why would you accept Onesimus back?

Asked of Philemon: How does your Christian faith change the way you see Onesimus?

In the second form of the interview approach, the group members decide what questions to ask. The group spends a few minutes formulating a huge list of questions they would like to ask of characters in the passage, and they then choose about six or eight of these to use. The leader should have two or three good questions to throw in when the full list of questions is being collected in case the group has not identified some important aspect of the passage. This ensures important content is discussed.

There are a number of things to be aware of when using this technique:

✦ The technique is only useful where the passage is a narrative or contains much of the author's personal viewpoint.

✦ Emphasise that the answers must come from the passage. This should allay the fear of younger Christians who feel they don't know much, and it deters people from 'making up answers' which have nothing to do with the text. It is important to select only questions which can actually be answered from the text.

✦ If you have someone in the group who is particularly obtuse or 'heretical', he or she is likely to lead a partner astray and should be paired with yourself or another strong Christian.

✦ There is a danger of meandering away from the topic. We usually eavesdrop on conversations, occasionally asking whether group members are dealing with the passage and actually answering the questions, and occasionally intervening if the pair is getting stuck or moving onto dangerous ground.

 EXAMPLE: Philippians 1:12–30

This passage is reasonably well-known but often people have difficulty expressing what it means. By having people answer questions as if they were Paul, they have to express his ideas in their own words.

Observation

Read Philippians 1:12–30 aloud. Set the scene by telling people that Paul is going to visit the group in ten minutes time in order for the group to interview him. Ask each individual to identify the questions he or she would like to ask him, noting the verse from which each question arises. Allow around five minutes for reading the passage again and developing questions.

Collect all the possible questions on butcher's paper, contributing the following questions (or others you have developed) during this time.

Verse 12: How can being in prison advance the gospel?

Verse 15: Don't motives matter at all in preaching? What about Galatians 1:8–9 and Philippians 3:18–19?

Verse 21: How can you say 'for me to live is Christ'? What do you mean?

Verse 27: What do you mean by 'conduct yourselves in a manner worthy…'? How do you actually do it?

Have the group select the six to eight questions in which they are most interested.

Tell the group that Paul is not able to come, but that they can try to work out what he would have answered by looking at what he wrote. Break into pairs and answer the questions by interviewing 'Paul'. Allow around 10–15 minutes. Remind people that they do not have to act, just answer the questions from the passage without using jargon. Get them to record any difficulties.

Interpretation

Reform the larger group and discuss the answers given to each question.

Consider the overall meaning and significance of the passage. Why did Paul write this passage?

Application

What should we do in response to this passage?

Pray.

---

10. SENTENCE ANALYSIS

This technique is excellent for passages with complex arguments. It works well with epistles where the arguments can be quite dense, and particularly with Paul's letters as he often gets carried away with his line of thought.

Sentence analysis involves detailed work with a passage. The object is to break down each sentence into its component parts and then to arrange these parts to indicate the relationship of ideas within the passage. You do not change the wording or punctuation of the passage, but simply arrange the elements of the passage according to the flow of ideas. The breakdown of the passage is called a flow chart. It is easiest explaining sentence analysis by showing an example. If your group can see it, it is easier to work out.

Romans 1:1–4 is a good example of a passage where sentence analysis really helps. It is actually one long sentence in the original Greek, so sentence analysis helps make it easier to understand by dividing up the flood of ideas.

1 Paul,
    a servant of Jesus Christ,
    called to be an apostle,
    set apart for the gospel of God,
        2 (the gospel) which he promised
            beforehand
            through his prophets
            in the holy Scriptures,
        3 the gospel concerning his Son,
            who was descended from David
                according to the flesh
        4 and was declared to be Son of God with power
            according to the spirit of holiness
                by resurrection from the dead,
        Jesus Christ our Lord

The way we explain this to people is that the first idea is on the left hand margin.

1 Paul,

This passage begins with an introduction to Paul. If there is a development of the first idea, then you offset it to the right. In this example, after his introduction, Paul states three things about himself.

    a servant of Jesus Christ,
    called to be an apostle,
    set apart for the gospel of God,

Paul then goes on to develop the idea 'gospel of God', so this is offset another place to the right.

        2 (the gospel) which he promised
            beforehand
            through his prophets
            in the holy Scriptures,
        3 the gospel concerning his Son,
            who was descended from David
                according to the flesh
        4 and was declared to be Son of God with power
            according to the spirit of holiness
                by resurrection from the dead,
        Jesus Christ our Lord

Paul proceeds to develop the idea of gospel of God by explaining that it was promised and that it was regarding God's Son. Verse 2 explores the fact that the gospel was promised, explaining that it was promised beforehand, it was promised through his prophets, and it was promised in the holy Scriptures. In verse 3, he explores the idea of Son and comments on three things: his human nature, his declaration as the Son of God, and his identity as Jesus. Look for words and phrases that are repeated, such as 'according to', and line them up underneath each other. Notice that 'declared to be' and 'by resurrection' also go together. It can be helpful to use different coloured highlighters to mark key words that go together.

When using sentence analysis with a group, you can either have the group develop the flow chart or you can prepare it in advance. Preparing the flow chart in advance saves time, while doing it as a group means the group works hard on the passage. (We always prepare a flow chart for ourselves when leading a study as an aid to understanding the passage).

If the group is given a copy of the flow chart, we conduct the study by having them underline or circle key ideas and repeated words before discussing the meaning of the passage as a whole. If the group has prepared the flow chart themselves we usually find that the basic observation, interpretation and application questions are adequate for discussion as they have already wrestled with the text as they prepared it. The example below combines sentence analysis and some discussion questions.

EXAMPLE: Galatians 6:1–5

Observation

Read Galatians 6:1–5 and then develop a flow chart of the passage by doing sentence analysis as a group. Each new idea or explanation is offset by one place. If there is a repetition of an idea then it is lined up under the phrase that made a similar point.

Discuss what people notice about the text. Use these questions to help if necessary:

Who is qualified to offer help?

What should we do?

How should we do it?

What personal preparation do we need?

What is the danger to us?

What principle for self-evaluation is presented here?

Does Paul contradict himself by saying 'carry each other's burden' and then 'carry your own load'?

Interpretation

What does this passage mean and why do you think Paul wrote it?

Application

What difference does this passage make to us?

Pray.

11. MAPPING

This is a technique we have used with great success. It involves drawing a map and recording what is happening, where. It is useful for narratives where the story develops during a journey or moves from one location to another. The aim is to consider how the plot develops, using the physical locations mentioned as reference points. This helps the group cover a large passage carefully while trying to understand the author's intent. The main questions are: 'How is the plot developing as we move from one location to another?', and 'What use is the writer making of references to various places?'

Mapping the Exodus narrative is a good activity in Bible study groups as we often meet people who think the journey actually required forty years. Mapping the journey highlights the fact that the people wandered as a consequence of their disobedience.

EXAMPLE: Mark 8:27–11:11

This whole passage is about Jesus' journey to Jerusalem and the significant things he taught. This is a long passage which should be studied in one go, as well as in smaller parts. (We have used this study as an overview before studying the smaller sections in detail.) The aim of the study is to understand Jesus' purpose on his final journey into Jerusalem, a major theme in Mark's Gospel. Use a Bible Atlas to draw an outline map of the area on butcher's paper before the study, and have it handy so that you can place the towns referred to.

Observation

Divide the passage into sections and allocate these to pairs or individuals: Mark 8:27–9:1; Mark 9:2–32; Mark 9:33–50; Mark 10:1–45; Mark 10:46–11:11.

Have each pair read their passage with the aim of being able to summarise the events for the rest of the group and answer the following questions:

> Where were the disciples and Jesus?
>
> What did Jesus teach?
>
> What did the disciples learn?

Draw on butcher's paper the places mentioned in the passage: Caesarea Philippi, Mt Hermon, Capernaum, Judea, Jordan River, Bethany and Jerusalem.

Have each pair report their findings to the rest of the group. Draw the journey first and then record on the map Jesus' teaching for the disciples at each place.

Discuss any passages that are hard to understand as you go along.

Interpretation

Ask the group to summarise Jesus' purpose for his teaching during the journey. What are the significant teachings and why would Jesus be teaching them? What difference does it make to the disciples? What difference should it make to us?

Application

What will you do differently as a result of this passage?

Pray.

12. LIST

This method involves making lists. Generally we ask participants to work in pairs and record all the references to a particular idea or word, or all the commands or instructions within a passage. A list helps people to observe a passage and see the repetition and main themes. It also assists in making links between ideas during interpretation. Once a list is developed, the group uses this as the basis for interpretation and application.

EXAMPLE: Colossians 3:1–17

The aim of this study is for people to be realistic about applying the lists in Colossians 3 to themselves.

Observation

Explain to the group the method being used.

Read Colossians 3:1–17 aloud.

Ask the group to record on the left hand side of their paper the list of things the Colossians are not to do from verses 5–11 (allow some space between each one).

Then in pairs write a jargon-free definition of each word. Be realistic and specific – do not allow trite Christian super-spiritualisms. Once everyone has done this, discuss any difficulties and share the definitions around the group.

Repeat the process with the things the Colossians are to do in verses 12–17.

Interpretation

As a group, discuss the key ideas and overall meaning of the passage.

What principles are there behind Paul's exhortation?

Conclude with a summary statement from verse 17 and encouragement from verses 3 and 4.

Application

Since we are in a similar situation to the Colossians, have people discuss (in pairs):

> Which one of these commands do they find most difficult?

> What specifically are they going to do about it?

If you think there is adequate trust in the group have them share their answers; your own honesty helps if you go first. If you are going to ask them to share publicly, you must warn them before they do the exercise, otherwise they could feel tricked and overexposed.

Pray for each other.

---

13. TABLE

Setting up a simple table can help a group observe the details of a passage. This is particularly useful for seeing the development of ideas or the correlation between them in a passage.

For example, Paul's epistles often explore the implications of being Christian. Ephesians 4:17–5:24 could be examined using this table:

	Description of status	Attitudes	Behaviours
Christian			
Non-Christian			

Having used a table to observe the passage, the interpretation and application would involve discussing the basic questions: What does the text mean? and How do we respond?

Example: Matthew 13:1-9, 18-23

Background

This is a well-known story and therefore requires work to keep the group focused. Since this and the later parables are about the kingdom of God, you need to clarify that during interpretation.

Observation

Read Matthew 13:1–9, 18–23. Have the group create a table based on the two passages. (The last column is to record whether the response is Christian or not).

Soil type	Response	Meaning	Christian or non-Christian?

Ask group members to share their completed table with the group. Discuss any questions or comments.

Interpretation

Consider the context of this parable, discuss why Jesus told it, and summarise the point of it.

Your group may find it difficult to determine whether the third group in the parable is Christian or not. Look for key words in the description of their response, and you may like to check the parallel passage in Mark and reliable Bible commentaries.

Application

In our times, what distinguishes the third group from the fourth group?

Discuss what response this passage requires. Ask people to consider where they and their friends are. Pray.

14. ROLE-PLAY

Members of your group identify with one set of characters in a passage, then present these characters to the rest of the group. This involves presenting their ideas and, if the need arises, actually defending them. We find that many people dislike role-plays. Therefore when explaining this technique, we don't actually call it a 'role-play'. We simply describe what the group is going to do.

Allocate characters in the narrative to sub-groups ('You four are Goliath and the Philistines; you three are David and the Israelites.'). Ask them to collect all the information they can about who they are and who they think God is. We ask them to create a team motto, which helps people read the passage carefully to truly understand the views of the people they represent. Each group presents its findings to the other half of the group.

This technique is particularly helpful in Old Testament narratives which feature multiple adversarial groups. It helps clarify what role each group plays and why the action happens as it does.

EXAMPLE: Daniel 2[21]

This chapter features a tussle between two world views, a situation not unlike the one in which we find ourselves today. A world view is made up of the ideas people have about themselves and others, human nature, the world and its purpose, and God.

Observation

Read Daniel 2.

Allocate the group into two opposing 'teams' with captains. One team represents Nebuchadnezzar and the astrologers; the other, Daniel and the Jews. Give each group time to identify and record the components of their world view, their understanding of God according to the text, and to create a motto or slogan for each team.

Have each team tell the rest of the group one aspect of their world view (from the text) until the lists are exhausted.

Have each team list the attributes of the God they believe in and what that God's actions in the world are. (Groups often find it more engaging if they talk about 'we believe...' rather than 'they believe...'.)

Discuss any questions or comments.

Interpretation

Why would this story be recorded? What purpose would the author have? What is the point of the event?

How do you think God would react to these world views? Why would he react that way? What particular aspects of God's character would cause him to be offended by the world views?

---

21. This study has been published in a fuller form by Karen Morris and Andrew Reid in *Kingdom of Dreams* (Sydney: St Matthias Press, 1997).

Application

Identify some of the opposing world views represented by the statements of people we know and our society in general. How could we respond to these world views?

How do you think God would react to these world views? Why would he react this way?

How do these world views affect us personally? What would you like to say in response to 'alternative' world views?

Pray.

15. LOGIC, FLOW, AND CAUSE AND EFFECT DIAGRAMS

These methods enable people to examine the development of an argument by drawing a diagram which indicates key ideas, examples, asides, and tangents. This process is most useful for unravelling complicated arguments – especially those that have numerous asides and apparent digressions.

Draw these diagrams with boxes and arrows. The boxes contain the ideas. The arrows indicate the flow of the logic. We go across for an aside or explanation, and down for progression in the argument. We break the passage into its main units, which will sometimes be whole chapters, and at other times just a sentence or phrase. Write one unit (or a short summary if it is a long unit) in each box.

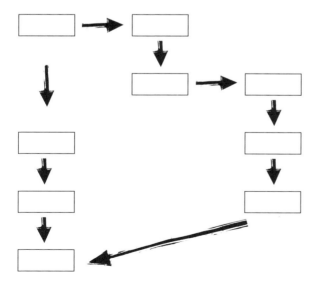

The process involves asking people to draw the connections between various ideas, and then discussing why they are connected in that particular way.

When developing these diagrams in a group, it can be helpful to hand out a page prepared with a box grid, into which people can insert information.

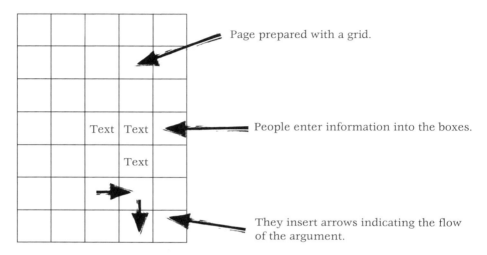

Page prepared with a grid.

People enter information into the boxes.

They insert arrows indicating the flow of the argument.

These diagrams appeal to those with 'mathematical' minds, who enjoy having things clearly laid out in sequence. Others might find them rigid and frustrating. Remember to use variety in your methodology to accommodate different learning styles.

Logic diagrams show the development of a writer's logic. They are particularly helpful with passages like Ephesians 3, where the first sentence ends in mid-air and appears to recommence at verse 7. A logic diagram shows how the passage fits together.

Flow diagrams are similar to logic diagrams, but do not necessarily plot the structure of the passage. Flow diagrams clarify the relationships between various ideas, and can be used to show the overall flow of an argument within a book. Look for connections such as 'therefore' and 'since' to see how the author builds the argument. Romans is one book where an understanding of the overall flow of the argument assists in understanding the parts. Many people study Romans in blocks without understanding the overall thrust of the book. Romans 1:18 begins an argument which continues through to the final chapters.

Cause and effect diagrams identify the linkages within a passage and show how one idea leads on to the next. Ephesians 4:11–16 is a great example of a short passage with a clear progression of ideas.

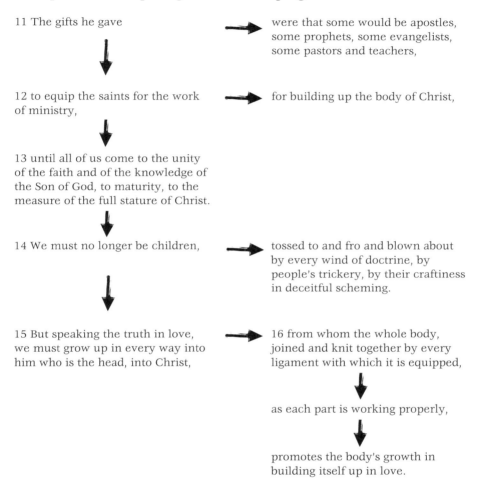

11 The gifts he gave → were that some would be apostles, some prophets, some evangelists, some pastors and teachers,

12 to equip the saints for the work of ministry, → for building up the body of Christ,

13 until all of us come to the unity of the faith and of the knowledge of the Son of God, to maturity, to the measure of the full stature of Christ.

14 We must no longer be children, → tossed to and fro and blown about by every wind of doctrine, by people's trickery, by their craftiness in deceitful scheming.

15 But speaking the truth in love, we must grow up in every way into him who is the head, into Christ, → 16 from whom the whole body, joined and knit together by every ligament with which it is equipped,

as each part is working properly,

promotes the body's growth in building itself up in love.

The cause and effect progression goes down the page, while asides and explanations go across. This outline makes it clear that the focus of this passage is Christian growth and maturity, with gifts being given to promote that growth and maturity.

In a group, the process is either to develop the diagram collectively, discussing it as it is developed, or individually, with people comparing their diagrams and the group discussing the differences. Having developed the diagram, the group discusses the general interpretation and application questions.

We tend to use logic diagrams for shorter passages and chapters, flow diagrams for large sections and whole books, and cause and effect for detailed passages.

 EXAMPLE: 2 Corinthians 11:1–15

This passage is part of a long continuous argument (2 Corinthians 10:1–13:10). It is good to read it in its entirety.

Observation

To understand this passage better we need to follow Paul's logic. Draw a logic diagram of the passage, summarising the ideas into boxes on the table below and drawing arrows indicating the connections. At times Paul goes off on a tangent that is left unfinished, and your diagram should indicate this. At other times Paul returns to a thought he had before, and this link should also be shown. Here is the beginning of the diagram to show you how:

Please put up with my silliness ⟶	I know you think you are already		
I am really concerned for you ⟶	I carefully united you with Christ, because you belong to him ⟶	But I'm concerned you might be deceived in your faith ⟶	You accept all sorts of lies from others, who are good speakers
			I am not inferior to them even though I am not a trained speaker

Interpretation

What questions or comments do you have about the passage?

As a group, summarise the main argument as briefly and clearly as you can. Leave out the tangents and asides.

What sort of emotions do you think Paul is feeling in this situation? Why is Paul reacting this way?

What do you think the situation is in Corinth when Paul is writing? What might be happening that is making Paul react this way?

Application

Have you ever been in a situation where you have reacted like Paul, or think you should have reacted the way Paul does? Explain to the group.

Have you ever been in a situation where you reacted like Paul, but realised later you shouldn't have? Explain to the group.

What guidelines would you make for yourself about reacting to situations?

Pray about the things you have learned in the study.

---

16. PLOT

This involves drawing a chart or graph to record one element in relation to another. This method can be used with people working in pairs to cover reasonably big slabs of text, or it can be used as a focal point for group discussion. It is particularly useful in Old Testament narrative where you need an overview to understand each individual story. Judges, Joshua, Kings and Chronicles could be studied using this method. You might ask the group to plot the variation in Israel's attitude to God and in God's attitude to Israel over time.

EXAMPLE: Exodus 15–17

Observation

Read Exodus 15:1–17:15. This passage immediately follows the rescue of Israel from Egypt. Draw a simple graph which plots Israel's attitude towards God over time, like the one on the following page.

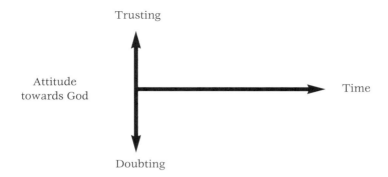

Have people identify verses which describe the Israelites' attitude to God. Mark these on the graph with a cross, including verse references. Discuss the pattern that emerges.

Interpretation

Identify the key theme of this passage, and discuss what it teaches us about God's faithfulness to his covenant.

Application

Discuss how we respond to this passage. Consider especially how easy it is to forget what God has done.

When have you been in a situation in which you grumbled against God? How would you do it differently as a result of this study?

Pray for each other.

17. KEY QUESTION

The key question approach is a way to study one aspect of a Bible character or a book of the Bible without having to study everything about the character or book. The leader prepares by formulating a question which will focus the group onto the area to be examined:

What is the source of Paul's joy in Philippians?

What are the proofs of salvation in 1 John?

What is the relationship between love and other gifts in 1 Corinthians 12–14?

You could compare it with a guided tour of a city. The guide takes you to see the parts of the city he or she thinks are interesting. The guide has shown you the city but, of course, there is much more to see. In Cairns, you could take a tour of the beaches, and another of the rainforest. Both would be legitimate tours, but each focuses on only one aspect of Cairns. In the same way, a key question helps you to study one aspect of a book or character in a creative and relevant way without being engrossed in all the details. As this method is deductive rather than inductive in essence, it is crucial that the key question identifies a genuine theme in the letter and not a secondary issue.

EXAMPLE: Mark's Gospel

Observation

Jesus' death has been identified as central to Christianity. Examine Mark's Gospel to determine if Jesus considered this to be true. The key question is:

How important does Jesus consider his death to be?

Allocate specific chapters for individuals or pairs to examine. Each sub-group works through their passage considering the key question and then reports back to the main group with their findings. A summary of the findings is recorded on butcher's paper for later referral during discussion.

Interpretation

Discuss the significance of Jesus' death to our understanding of Christianity.

Application

Discuss the implications of this to our faith, especially focusing on the issue of evangelism and cross-cultural mission.

Pray for each other.

18. QUESTIONS

This method of observation is the most common in Bible study. In our experience it is also the least interesting since it has been overused and is often little more than a comprehension checking exercise. If you do use this technique then it is useful to acquire some basic skills in questioning.

Firstly, there are two types of questions: open questions and closed questions. As these two require different types of answers, it is important to use the right one when asking a question. People will generally answer the question according to how it was asked! Open questions are for obtaining information. They cannot be answered with a simple 'yes' or 'no'. Closed questions on the other hand can be answered by 'yes' or 'no'. Closed questions can be used to affirm or deny information, but they are not designed to generate new information. The difference between open and closed questions can be understood by considering these questions:

How is Jesus described?	Is Jesus the Son of God?
What must someone do to be saved?	Are we saved by works?
When will Christ return?	Do we know when Jesus will return?
Where is Jesus now?	Is Jesus in heaven?
Who is Paul?	Is Paul an apostle?
What does that mean?	Do you understand?

The questions on the left are open questions; they require more than a simple yes or no. The questions on the right however are closed questions; they can be answered using yes or no.

We do not maintain that group leaders should only use open questions. It is appropriate to use both open and closed questions at different times, depending on what sort of information you need. As leader, you must decide which type of question will generate the type of answer required.

Secondly, remember that one question should lead to others as the answer is explored and considered. This is where probing questions become important. Some examples of these are:

Why do you say that?

Where do you see that in the text?

Could you say that in other words for us?

What do others in the group think about that suggestion?

Thirdly, it is important to allow people enough time to think about what has been asked. We often see people answer their own question, or ask a second on top of the first, when the group is still considering its answer. As it is a great temptation for leaders to give 'little sermons' when answering their own questions, the leader should rephrase the question rather than give the answer.

Fourthly, it is very easy for questions to become patronising or banal. The leader must work hard at asking questions which are actually interesting and worth the effort of answering.

The fifth point should be apparent by now. Any question you ask as a leader should be part of the three main questions which a Bible study must address:

✦ What does the text actually say?

✦ What does the text mean?

✦ How do we respond to what the text means?

 EXAMPLE

There are numerous question/answer type studies published. We suggest you examine a study guide you have recently used to see how well it helps people do observation, interpretation, and application. Count how many questions can be answered without your Bible. Look at the introduction to see if it pre-empted the passage. Does it use open and closed questions appropriately? Consider whether the study focused on understanding the passage, or simply used it as a springboard into discussing a topic.

19. SWEDISH METHOD

This simple method of observation is very easy to use and great for a group that is new to Bible study. Each member reads the chosen passage and then approximately ten minutes is set aside for individual thinking and study.

Everyone is provided with a card or piece of paper, down the side of which they draw three symbols:

Question mark   Light bulb   Arrow

At the question mark, group members make a note of any word, expression, or verse which they would question, either because they don't understand it or because they don't agree with it.

The light bulb stands for those thoughts which, after the passage has been considered several times, throw light on the rest of the passage or some personal concern.

At the arrow, a note is made of the point which most sharply challenges or pricks the conscience.

Members need not feel that they must write something beside each symbol.

At the end of the time, the group comes together again and each member has a chance to comment on the notes made. Then follows general discussion, questions, sharing and the development of thoughts and insights. The leader should be sure that the meaning of the passage is not lost in the discussion, and time should be left for a short summary at the end.

EXAMPLE

Observation

Explain to the group what they will be doing. Give each person a sheet of paper and ask him or her to draw the three symbols down the side of the page.

Read your chosen passage and then allow participants 5–10 minutes on their own to complete the observation activity.

Ask members to share their responses to both the question mark and the light bulb, progressing through the passage verse by verse. Discuss these comments as they arise.

Interpretation

As a group, identify the key themes of the passage and discuss what the passage as a whole means.

Application

Have participants share what they wrote alongside the arrow symbol. Ensure these comments are consistent with the overall meaning of the passage.

Give people time to decide what they will do in response to the passage, then share this, and pray as a group.

20. IONA METHOD

This method is for groups with up to ten members who have already developed good skills at observation. It is similar to the Swedish method, but does not provide a framework for observation. The leader must be properly prepared, to ensure the passage is fully understood. The passage to be studied is reproduced on sheets of paper, to allow notes to be made and questions to be recorded.

The leader distributes the text to members of the group and asks them to read silently for up to ten minutes, considering what significance the passage appears to have. People can also be invited to note any unclear or perplexing parts of the passage.

After the time for reading, the leader invites each member in succession to share, briefly, items of significance arising from the passage. Each person is given opportunity to speak or not to speak as desired and there should be an encouraging climate to promote this. The whole group could keep a brief record of comments or questions to facilitate later discussion (keeping track of verse numbers). It is important that all members have an opportunity to comment on the passage before general discussion begins.

After these individual contributions have been received, general discussion can proceed, guided by the comments and questions raised. At the conclusion of the study time, it is helpful for the leader or another group member to sum up the passage, checking that the three basic questions have been answered (What does the text say? What does the text mean? How do we respond to the text?).

21. MANUSCRIPT DISCOVERY AS A METHOD OF BIBLE STUDY[22]

This method of Bible study is not an observation technique for a single meeting, but rather a process for observation, interpretation and application over a longer period. We have included it here for your consideration because it is a great way to get into Scripture as a group.

You might like to use manuscript discovery (MD) on a Bible study weekend away. It involves helping an individual to discover the overall meaning and purpose of one book of the Bible, or a large section of one book of the Bible. The text of Scripture is presented on sheets of paper without the usual chapters and verses (as were the originals, although we use English rather than Greek or Hebrew). We call it a manuscript. The group works through the manuscript identifying themes, key ideas and structure. The aim is to understand the manuscript as a document in its own right.

---

22. This description of Manuscript Discovery was originally developed by Rosemary Pidgeon and is used with her permission.

Readers see how particular themes are developed throughout the book and how specific sections and questions can be understood in the light of the whole text.

Ideally, the leaders should have had some experience with MD, and preferably some training, though this is hard to come by. Leading an MD group can be quite a challenge, as it is tempting to answer questions before you have really come to grips with the book as a whole. The leader is more of a study coordinator than a guru with all the answers. The leader is a learner too.

The leader deals with questions by getting group members to investigate further by themselves, directing them to consider other sections of the text and encouraging them to see specific points in their context. Leaders must constantly make it clear that the authority in determining what the text is saying is the text itself. All comments must be supported by data in the text.

How to do manuscript discovery

Choose a book or section which can be dealt with in the time available – you could not do justice to John's Gospel in a weekend! Print out your selection with wide margins and double-spaced lines. Use page and line numbers (mark every fifth line – 5, 10, 15...). Do not show paragraphs, chapter or verse numbers, or especially headings. You will soon get used to referring to page and line numbers. Bible translations are subject to copyright, so you may need to apply for copyright permission. A printout from a computer Bible is ideal – with verse numbers and paragraphing removed – but again check that you have permission to use it.

✦ Ban Bibles, commentaries and Bible dictionaries. (These may be used for reference towards the end of your study.) Only use the manuscript!

✦ Divide people into groups of about six, with one or two leaders.

✦ Begin your group by introducing the method and its purpose, explaining that members will spend time in individual study and report back to the group at designated times.

✦ Hand out the manuscript and get people to read it through individually in one sitting, without marking it at all. Make a finishing time – you should have worked out how long it takes – even though some slow readers may find this hard.

✦ In your first group session after reading the manuscript, ask members for their initial responses to the text as a whole and record these on a large sheet of paper (keep this sheet for comparison later on). Do not encourage specific discussion at this stage, just general impressions of and reactions to the text.

✦ In their second reading of the text, encourage group members to mark the manuscript. They should underline things that strike them, or words and ideas that recur many times, or questions raised by what they are reading. The second group session deals with these more specific responses and questions. Questions may be of any type: broad, specific, questions of application or interpretation. Record these questions on a piece of paper (noting their page and line number).

✦ If you have plenty of time, group members may like to read the text again, attempting to break it up into its sections. However, try to do this fairly quickly without getting bogged down in details. Another large sheet of paper could be pinned up for people to record their breakdown of the text. These may be fairly different, reflecting members' developing interest in particular ideas and themes.

✦ The next stage is for members to select a theme to study. They will have read the manuscript through many times by now and their interest may have been aroused by a particular idea of the writer. The themes decided on may overlap. This can be quite useful in group discussion, helping the group see the overall purpose of the writer.

To do a theme study, members read the text through, yet again, marking all references to the theme, both direct and implied. At the same time or at the conclusion of this reading, make a list of these references and then in columns alongside record such things as: who said it and to whom; the context (setting, surrounding ideas); questions raised and possible meanings. Only when all references have been exhausted should an overall understanding of the theme be attempted, considering such things as:

What would it have meant to the first readers?

How does it fit into the overall purpose of the book?

What are the questions it raises for Christians today?

How should it be understood and applied today?

Most of this can be done individually, with members chatting to each other about any questions. At certain regular times, the group should come together so that members can share with each other their progress (or lack of it). Leaders should be aware there may be some frustration. This can be constructive in the long term as individuals are encouraged to re-investigate the text to find out answers. Always work from the text, trying to grapple with what it is saying. Do not initially bring to it ideas from other parts of the Bible.

✦ Towards the end of your MD, members may like to use a reference Bible, especially if there are many Old Testament references, or a Bible dictionary to assist with particularly difficult parts.

✦ In your final group session, members present their findings to the group. The initial response and question sheets could be re-examined briefly, so progress in understanding can be seen. Welcome contributions on how individuals reacted to the MD method, as well as dealing with the overall purpose of the writer, difficulties still outstanding (others may be able to help here) and applications for today.

MD is exciting and rewarding, but like other methods of Bible study, it is only useful as we apply the message of Scripture in our lives. Paul Byer, who developed MD, wrote, 'our understanding of Scripture will be opened or blocked, more by our obedience than by our study methods. The goal then of every Bible study is to act on what we hear'.[23]

Assisting poor readers

We have occasionally been asked whether using these techniques requires too high a level of reading ability. We don't think so. In fact, we think it is far easier for most people to have an activity to do and then something concrete to look at afterwards, than simply discuss abstract ideas in a group. Having something physical to refer back to during discussion seems to act as a safety net for many people, and we often find people pointing to ideas written on butcher's paper as the study progresses.

A friend of ours conducts Bible studies with people who are not skillful readers. He agrees that activities help people understand the Bible. He says people in his groups find it easier to study the Bible when they have something to do and something to look at.

---

23. Quoted by Rosemary Pidgeon in an unpublished article.

If you have people in your group who cannot read, always make sure the passage is read out loud. These people often have highly developed memories. If there are people who struggle to read, always announce the passage a week in advance so they can read it for themselves at home.

A comment on study guides

We are often asked about the usefulness of published study guides and which ones to use. Generally, we prefer to write our own material. We would encourage you to write your own as well.

Most published studies are based on the comprehension question technique, and many use a passage as a jumping off point rather than the focus of the study. They stretch a text in order to develop an idea.

Study guides can become a problem if the aim of the group becomes to complete the questions rather than to understand the passage. It is OK not to answer every question. Many discussions have been cut short so the group could move on in order to complete the questions. This is a problem! **A study guide is an aid to understanding a passage. The passage should never become an aid for completing the study guide.**

Given that, good quality study guides are useful if they help to ensure the quality of your content when doing thematic studies. This is our rule of thumb: If while we are standing in the bookshop we can answer the first three questions of any study without looking at the passage then it is not worth buying. Studies published by Aquila Press, Inter-Varsity Press, Navigators and St Matthias Press are often good in their handling of Scripture.

A fallacy about study guides is that they do not require as much preparation as a normal study. Our experience is they take as much time to modify for your own use as writing a study from scratch does.

Most published studies are intended for use in sessions of 60 to 90 minutes, while many groups have only 45 to 60 minutes available. The group can easily find itself consistently running out of time and consequently failing to apply the passage. We suggest you work through the study yourself in order to check that it deals well with the passage and focuses on its central theme. Then prepare a leader's version by deciding which questions you will answer and which ones you will ignore.

Thematic Bible studies

Thematic or topical Bible studies are exactly what the name suggests. The leader prepares a study which looks at what the Bible says about a particular theme or topic. The usual approach is to look at verses relevant to the issue, discuss what they mean and then draw them together into a conclusion or summary. The verses can be found by looking in a concordance, and many people use a chapter of a book or a sermon as the basis for their material. Books such as *The fight*, *Know the truth*, and the *I believe in...* series are good.

Thematic studies are helpful as they bring together material from all over the Bible and give an overall view. However, they have the potential to be misleading or unbalanced, depending on what is included or left out. It is possible to write a thematic study which proves that Christians should fly using verses such as 'rising up on wings like eagles' and 'Jesus ascending into heaven'. You should see if you can do it! This is obviously dangerous.

Summary

Group Bible study involves answering three basic questions:

✦   What does the text actually say?

✦   What does the text mean?

✦   How do we respond to what the text means?

Your role as leader is to assist the group as they answer these questions, acting like an African Safari guide. Ensure the group wrestles with the text and reaches the point where the members can confidently answer each question. Our goal is to equip people so they can return to this passage, or another, and study and understand the word of God.

Obviously 'learning from the Bible in groups' is done corporately. The next chapter will help you consider how to 'develop group life'.

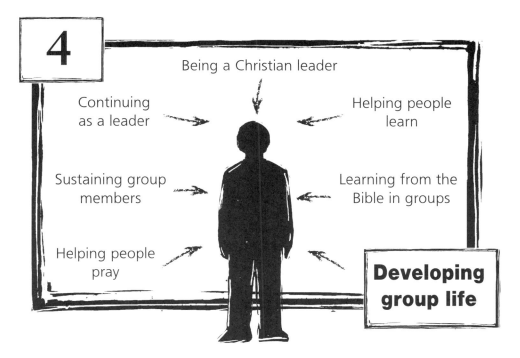

Being a Christian leader

Continuing as a leader

Helping people learn

Sustaining group members

Learning from the Bible in groups

Helping people pray

Developing group life

Ten years ago Karen was in a group that was wonderful. The leaders obviously loved and cared for the group members and the members felt the same. Their life as a group was strong, warm, and fun. They studied the Bible with great fervour and enjoyment. They looked forward to each meeting and only missed evenings when they had absolutely no choice. This group has become the standard for groups we have run since then.

As we have learned about helping groups grow and develop we have labelled the processes of that model group. This chapter provides labels, frameworks and models to apply to your own groups and your own history. We look at effective groups, the changes groups go through over time, the optimum size of a group, processes for establishing and ending a group, and other elements of group life.

Sometimes we refer to a group as 'them', and sometimes as 'it'. This is because a group is a collection of individuals (them) and yet also develops an identity of its own (it). This second phenomenon is called 'synergy'. Sometimes, the group experience brings out the best in people. The potential in the group is more than the sum of the individual members. This is positive synergy. At other times, the individuals fail to combine effectively, and the group actually restricts the members within it. This is negative synergy.

Rod was once asked to take over the leadership of a group in difficulty. The thing he noticed immediately was that the group had a personality different from that which the individual members wanted. Individually, the group members were keen, enthusiastic Christians who wanted to grow and wanted to help each other grow. But the group was not working. It had developed a personality which was preventing the members from achieving their goals.

Since then we have noted that, over time, groups develop a personality which is a function of all the people in them and how they relate. Some groups seem serious, others frivolous. Some groups seem vibrant and energetic, others tired and listless. Some groups seem purposeful and focused, others seem lost and confused. This personality can either help or hinder a group's progress in achieving its goal.

With Rod's 'group in difficulty', the way ahead was for the group members to examine the group's personality and decide what sort of group they wanted and were committed to working for. The process for doing this will be discussed later under 'Group norms'.

Elements of effective groups

Think about groups you have been in – both good and bad. List some of their characteristics.

As you begin a group, it is helpful to understand what makes a good group good and a bad group bad. There are seven commonly identified elements of an effective group.

1. Clarity of purpose and expectations

Groups that function well contain members who understand where they are going and why they are going there. They agree with this purpose and are committed to working towards it. This implies that group members have probably helped develop the purpose statement. In groups which lack this consensus, there is a fundamental disunity. People join together for various reasons and constantly seek to shift the group towards a goal to which others in the group are not necessarily committed. In a Bible study group, our purpose is to help each other understand the Bible and apply it to our lives in order for us to grow as Christians.

2. Understanding of interdependence

In order for a group to be effective, it is essential that the members recognise the significance of the relationship between themselves and the other members of the group. They must also recognise the importance of each member and what he or she can contribute to the life of the group. The members of an effective group understand their interdependence. They recognise their need for each other. If some members consider others to be unnecessary, or unable to make a valuable contribution, the group will quickly develop problems. These attitudes will be reflected in group discussions and relationships. In a Bible study group we are interdependent. We are Christian brothers and sisters who come together in order to help each other know and love our Lord more fully.

3. Trust and respect

Trust and respect is crucial for the wellbeing of a group. Christians must agree that each group member needs to trust and respect the other members. It is part of loving people well! It fosters participation and a willingness to disclose significant things to the group, and is therefore essential to good group functioning. Where trust and respect are missing, a group will often become dysfunctional. It will slip into superficiality and pretence as group members discuss only what is 'safe', and only say what is 'acceptable'.

Trust and respect are developed slowly over the life of a group, and can be destroyed by a senseless comment over supper. People usually join a group with a degree of trust, based on their opinion of the leader and the assumption that those in the group have good intentions. However, this trust has to be confirmed by the group proving to be trustworthy over time. Most people risk small amounts of self-disclosure in order to see whether the group can be trusted with the more intimate concerns which are difficult to share. If the group proves trustworthy, the level of trust and risk-taking increases.

As leaders, we can help this process by taking risks ourselves. We can share our concerns, fears and anxieties with the group so they see us as willing to trust them. Trusting acts are just as important as trustworthy acts in helping a group develop.

A thoughtless joke or snigger in response to a statement can prevent a person from contributing again and ruin his or her trust of the group. The leader must act to set guidelines to be observed when people are contributing. While put-downs and smart comments may initially cause people to laugh, they are unhelpful to the healthy development of the group.

The response to one person can affect the way others in the group contribute. A person can easily think 'If they laughed at Peter when he said that, then they would certainly have laughed at me for what I was about to say!' Consequently, it is important to acknowledge and value a person's contribution to a group discussion, even when it is wrong. As leader you need to help people understand the truth, but your first response should always indicate respect for their contributions.

4. Challenge and safety

Healthy group life is a combination of challenge and safety. People need to be challenged in order to move forward. They need to be encouraged, even pushed, out of their comfort zones in order to see things differently, consider new ideas and try new behaviours. However, in order for this to happen they need a safe environment which provides encouragement, support and acceptance. If there is too much challenge, people will withdraw. If there is too little challenge, they stagnate and grow complacent. If there is too much safety, again the group stagnates. If there is too little safety, the group retreats. As leaders, we need to manage the balance between challenge and safety so that people are challenged to grow while at the same time feeling supported, encouraged and cared for.

5. Open and clear communication

Bible study groups are about talking. We listen at church, we read in our quiet time, but we talk at Bible study. Consequently, open and clear communication is crucial in the life of a Bible study group. It is our conviction that communication is essential for both learning and relationship: the central elements of Bible study groups. Without good communication, we cannot really help each other fully as we do not understand the other person's concerns or insights. For a deeper exploration of communication, we recommend *Why don't people listen?* by Hugh Mackay (Sydney: Pan, 1994).

6. Cohesion and balanced participation

A group must be one integrated whole rather than a loose affiliation of subgroups. Within the group there is a need for all to make a contribution without one or two members dominating. While it is appropriate that groups give special attention to individuals as they go through particular trials and difficulties, we believe it is unhelpful for a group to focus continually on the needs of one or two people at the expense of others. In some groups, the leader may dominate by always talking and not giving others a chance to contribute. In other groups a particular member may consume all the group's attention by being especially needy or verbose. Either of these is a problem.

There are some people who are not actually suitable for Bible study group membership. These people, who can be domineering of others or insatiable in their need for support, can actually extinguish a group by their constant need for attention. We are not suggesting that you do not seek to minister to these people.

> **We listen at church, we read in our quiet time, but we talk at Bible study.**

Rather, we believe they are better cared for by one-to-one discipleship and nurture instead of Bible study group participation.

This is a difficult issue. Our mandate from Christ is to love the unlovely and care for those who are outcasts in society. Consequently, a group may decide to care for someone who has particular needs. We suggest you limit the number of such people to one or two, and that you take care to ensure that ministering to them does not overwhelm yourself and the other members of the group.

7. Achievement and recognition

Gaining a goal and celebrating it is immensely important in groups. However, in Bible study groups it can be difficult to determine the achievement of a goal. Spiritual growth is difficult to quantify. Therefore we suggest that leaders run the group so that it is obvious when milestones are passed. This might mean finishing a book of the Bible and having a celebratory dinner. It might mean celebrating individual achievements such as finishing projects at work, completing subjects, changing jobs, overcoming difficulties. People's birthdays are also obvious opportunities for celebrating. The purpose is to help the group feel they are making progress towards their goal.

Sometimes a group will get bogged down in a series of studies which goes on for months on end, or in one particular study which stretches over multiple weeks. This is a problem as it creates the impression of making no progress at all. Our advice is to limit a series of studies to six to eight weeks and never to stretch a study over more than two meetings. If you wish to tackle a long book we suggest you plan to do it in stages. For example, you might study John's Gospel in three stages: six weeks on the overall narrative of the book, followed by a dinner; six weeks on the discourses of Jesus, followed by a break (either one week of prayer or a short series on another book); concluding with a series on the 'I am' statements of Jesus.

We also find it helpful to have a half-yearly review of where we have gone as a group and what we have learned. This highlights the progress the group has made during that time. Keep a book listing all the group's prayer points and review it every six months. This can be a great encouragement.

The group life bubble

This simple model ties together the issues of trust and respect, challenge and safety, and open and clear communication.

Consider the life of a group as a bubble.

Dented bubble

Some things will dent the bubble. It could be a joke about homosexuals over supper which indicates to the person struggling with homosexuality that the group cannot be trusted with that issue, or a discussion which ends in tears when the group disagrees.

No-go areas

The group or individuals then put a safety fence around particular issues because they do not trust the group or they do not want a past hurt to resurface. These issues become no-go areas in the life of the group.

Safe area

Over time, these no-go areas occupy a larger and larger portion of the group's relationship bubble, so that there are few issues which the group can freely discuss. Sadly, we suspect one of the reasons some Bible studies only deal with observation and interpretation is that there is not enough trust to attempt application.

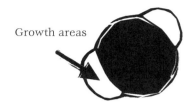

Growth areas

The alternative to this process is the growing bubble. Here, an issue which could have become a no-go area is shared with the group, and actually becomes the cause of greater understanding and deeper trust.

Growing safe areas

These groups, rather than slowly dying through the restrictions of no-go areas, flourish as people learn more about each other and help each other to live in response to God's Word. A growing range of topics is safe for the group to discuss. In these groups, application is often gutsy and challenging as people feel free to express and struggle with the concerns in their lives.

The size of a small group

The number of members is an important initial decision. It will affect all the interactions in the group for the rest of the group's life.

We recommend ten members as the ideal size. Most group literature identifies twelve members as the upper limit for an effective small group. The reasons are:

1. The number of potential interpersonal relationships in a group increases with every new member

In any group the number of possible relationships is the result of each person relating to every other person and subgroup. In a group with five members it is possible to draw all the relationships in this way:

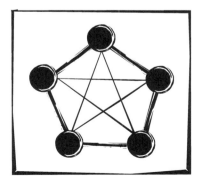

Imagine what a similar diagram would look like with fifteen people. As the group increases in size the number of potential relationships becomes more and more difficult to manage.

2. Every additional member increases the diversity of goals and expectations, with conflicting needs and values

Each additional member in a group brings his or her own intentions, expectations, needs and values. Having more than twelve in a group means that many of these things will not be heard. It increases the number of individual backgrounds and development stages. People will become frustrated or disappointed with the group as it fails to live up to their hopes.

3. Increasing the number of members results in reduced participation time per person, and increases the time it takes to perform tasks and discuss issues

Air time and process time are significant concepts for Bible study groups. Air time is the amount of time available for each member of the group to contribute. If a group of twelve meets for two hours, that means each person has only ten minutes to speak. As you increase the size of the group the number of minutes per person decreases. Process time refers to the amount of time it takes to do a task. An example is prayer time. If each member of a group takes three minutes to share prayer concerns and then a further two minutes to pray, every additional member will add five minutes to the prayer time. This means a group of six will take half an hour to pray, while a group of twelve members actually requires an hour for prayer. Even a simple thing like sharing the answer to a question will take longer when the group grows. Both decreased air time and increased process time can be annoying for group members. They can become frustrated and bored as things seem to take forever to happen, and opportunities to contribute or participate become increasingly rare.

4. More people means reduced physical space and comfort

Very few people have lounge rooms that can hold more than twelve people. Physical space and comfort are an important part of group functioning. Larger groups experience difficulty in hearing conversation, and difficulty in reading non-verbals due to limited eye contact. It is easy to misinterpret a person's comments by failing to see the smile as he or she speaks or the wink to the person just addressed.

5. Additional members means an increased gap between fast and slow workers, and creates difficulty coordinating member contributions

Trying to remember everyone's learning differences is extraordinarily difficult, let alone trying to accommodate them within the life of the group. If you are trying to be a gatekeeper, giving some people more time to speak and others less, you must limit the number of members. It is also harder for members to get the attention of the discussion leader if he or she is looking at fourteen other faces instead of ten.

6. It is difficult to care for a group of more than twelve

As Bible study groups have a pastoral agenda in most settings, it is appropriate to limit group size to ensure that the leader is not overwhelmed by the load and that the group is not so large that individuals begin to be overlooked.

Considering all these elements, we believe that once a group goes beyond twelve members, the size of the group actually begins to limit the group's ability to accomplish its goal effectively. Therefore our advice is to keep the size of a group between eight and twelve. The lower limit means you can still function as a group if there are a number of people away. The upper limit helps to maintain the sanity of the leader and the effectiveness of the group.

Group development

 Think about groups you have been in. Are there patterns to the way they develop? What stages do they go through?

Groups are like children – they grow and change all the time. They go through infancy, childhood, adolescence, adult maturity and old age. As a group changes it requires different things from the people who are looking after it.

A newborn baby and a teenager have completely different needs, and the interaction with their parents is also very different. You do not care for an infant in the same way you care for a teenager. To attempt to do so creates a whole range of problems and difficulties.

In this section, we look at how a group changes over time and what is required of you as a leader during each phase. The most useful model is one described by Tuckman in the early seventies and developed by Watson, Vallee and Mulford.[1] We use Tuckman's model because it is clear and the stages are memorable.

The model describes the life of a group as a series of phases. These are not necessarily linear, because for a variety of reasons a group can go back to an earlier stage, but they do describe how the emphasis changes within a group.

The labels are:

The rhyming helps you to remember it.

Forming

This first stage involves all the processes of bringing a group together. The members do not know each other and are assessing whether they will actually be able to be part of the group. They are looking for assurance that they can belong, and will behave in ways that begin to develop relationships and security in the group. The following table explains:[2]

Stage one – Forming			
Major emphasis		**Typical behaviour**	
Personal and interpersonal area	**Task area**	**Personal and interpersonal area**	**Task area**
Concern about inclusion, belonging, rejection, acceptance.	Concern with orientation to the task.	Polite, cautious, avoids conflict.	Asks questions such as: What are we supposed to do? What are our goals?

1.   H. J. Watson, J. M. Vallee and W. R. Mulford, *Structured experiences and group development* (Canberra: Curriculum Development Centre, 1980).
2.   Watson, Vallee and Mulford, 2.

Do you remember experiences of joining a group and feeling anxious, uncertain and tense? The questions in your mind were about the goal and purpose of the group. The role of the leader in such a group is to nurture and assure. The leader needs to smooth the process of relationship building with the group, as well as get the programme underway. This group is like a child – not because the members are naive or ignorant but because they need care and concern from the people involved. This stage is vital for establishing a foundation of trust so that the group is sustained through later stages.

Storming

The storming phase is where people cease to be excessively polite and begin to act more like their normal selves. This is the result of growing confidence that they belong to this group and have some say in the direction and processes involved. They begin to question rules that have been laid down, and some conflict may emerge as people spread their wings:[3]

Stage two – Storming			
Major emphasis		Typical behaviour	
Personal and interpersonal area	Task area	Personal and interpersonal area	Task area
Concern about power, control, status, authority, stress.	Concern with rules, agenda, organisation.	Conflict, power struggles, criticism.	Asks questions such as: What are the rules? How are we to be evaluated?

This group begins to seem like a teenage child to the unsuspecting leader. You began with a great group where everybody related really well and now there is conflict from a range of sources. The informed leader recognises this as simply another stage and works at providing freedom for discussion of rules, agenda and organisation, while still keeping some control of the group.

We are told that the parents of teenagers need to maintain a careful balance between being flexible and providing security and certainty.

---

3.   Watson, Vallee and Mulford, 2.

This seems to be good advice for the group leader with a storming group!

Norming

This stage delivers some peace after the storming phase. The young adult is emerging from the traumas of adolescence, and peace returns to the household. The group at this stage are really developing their normal operating procedures. They are cementing norms for the group:[4]

Stage three – Norming			
Major emphasis		Typical behaviour	
Personal and interpersonal area	Task area	Personal and interpersonal area	Task area
Concern about affection, groupness, open-mindedness, listening.	Data flows.	Cohesion, members think more of the group, joking occurs, team spirit builds.	Sharing information, willingness to change, win/win attitudes.

The norms set up during the opening stages begin to bear fruit during this phase. If poor norms were set in the forming stage, this is when they become obvious. (Refer to the later section in this chapter on establishing norms.) Groups in this stage start to feel settled and comfortable. They are beginning to be productive. The leader can begin to relinquish control over the group since they are now beginning to be responsible for themselves. The group is becoming willing to care for others and facilitate the process of Bible study.

Performing

The performing stage is when the group is functioning at its optimum. It is very settled and secure. The members are all contributing well and seek the good of others as well as of the whole group:[5]

---

4.   Watson, Vallee and Mulford, 2.
5.   Watson, Vallee and Mulford, 3.

Stage four – Performing			
Major emphasis		Typical behaviour	
Personal and interpersonal area	Task area	Personal and interpersonal area	Task area
Concern about interdependence and independence, high commitment, warmth, freedom.	Concern with problem-solving in a creative and self-renewing way.	Agrees to disagree.	Adapts to change, gives support, no complacency.

The group at this stage can be likened to the mature adult. They have developed the skills they need to function well in the world and have opportunities to use them. They are getting on with life. The leader of this group has some freedom. The group are able to take responsibility for themselves and others.

Mourning

Mourning is the last stage of a group. The members are beginning the process of separation from each other and are feeling grief over the impending lack of contact. They are reacting to the leader, especially if the leader is involved in the decision to end the group. They are also attempting to prolong contact and engineer reunions:[6]

Stage five – Mourning			
Major emphasis		Typical behaviour	
Personal and interpersonal area	Task area	Personal and interpersonal area	Task area
Concern about disengagement from relationship.	Concern with confusion about feelings.	Increased conflict and anger at the leader, conversely increased warmth between group members.	Breakdown of group skills, lethargy, frantic attempts to work well.

---

6. Watson, Vallee and Mulford, 3.

A group at this stage needs careful attention from the leader. The leader resumes responsibility after the period of reduced accountability during norming and performing. The leader needs to ensure that farewells are made in a healthy and comforting way. As with the death of a person, it is easier when there has been adequate time to say all the things you wanted to say. Sudden or unexpected endings are stressful both with human life and with groups.

Progress through the stages

As stated earlier, groups do not work through the phases in a linear manner. Various factors affect their progress.

One significant factor is the first meeting. If this meeting enables people to feel secure and have a clear understanding of the direction they are taking, the stress of the forming stage is reduced. It may be that a group can move through forming in one meeting. On the other hand it could take much longer if the group norms are not clearly established.

Another factor that can affect the stage of the group is the loss or gain of members. If a new member joins, the group will regress at least one level. If more than one person joins, the group needs to be considered as being in the forming stage again. You will be pleased to know that progress can be made more quickly, but there is always the regression first.

A leader can actually use this regression to the group's advantage. We always follow an introductory procedure for new members. This involves people telling the new member something about themselves and then telling them something about the group. The first is obvious, the second is not so obvious but can be quite fun. We ask the group to record on pieces of paper three things about the group the newcomer should know. If there are rules or standard procedures then use this time to inform the newcomer of these.

Usually, the group tells the newcomer lots of the important things about the group as well as some of the quite funny things. In a group we were leading, one person told the newcomers they could use anything in our house except the two special bottles of wine in the wine rack. Another member told the group joke, and a third showed them where the mugs, coffee and milk were. By the time we had spent half an hour they were thoroughly informed and the group had affirmed their identity as well as incorporating the newcomers.

If, on the other hand, people are leaving or the group is finishing, it is also important to acknowledge this. Various activities to inform each member of his or her contribution to the group are useful. A really simple one is to pin a sheet of paper to each person's back, and hand out felt pens so that each person can write on every other person's sheet. The comments should include things they have appreciated or enjoyed about the other person.

In the sections called 'Starting the group well' and 'Finishing well', there are other ideas for activities you could use at these crucial times in a group's life.

Use the model of group life to adjust your behaviour in light of the development of the group. Each stage requires different input and has its own joys and difficulties. In the following section we offer suggestions about how to establish the group well so that each stage is as smooth as possible.

Establishing group norms

When Karen was young, her little brothers played soccer. They were very funny to watch because, as five year olds, they did not have much of an idea of the positions or tactics of the game. Consequently, they ran all over the field like soldier crabs. No matter how much the coach explained, wherever the ball was, that was where every member of both teams was. The normal behaviour of the teams was to chase the ball everywhere. As they grew up, they began to understand the idea of positions and so played differently. The normal behaviour changed and became more sophisticated.

In every Bible study group there are patterns of acceptable behaviour and expectations from the group members. These patterns or norms can be determined deliberately by the group and the leader; or develop by default. Much like in the five year olds' soccer team, whether the leader acknowledges the norms is irrelevant, they will exist.

In a group of adults it is appropriate to set aside time to work on developing norms during the forming stage of the group. This process gives all participants the opportunity to express their views and have input into how the group develops. The group participates in its own development.

For example, we led a group where the first week was spent discussing what we wanted and how we were going to achieve it. By the third week everybody was referring to it not as 'Karen and Rod's group', or 'the church home group I go to', but as 'our group'. This enabled the group to develop very quickly.

A basic rule is that something is always happening to the norms of a group, whether it be positive or negative, obvious or hidden. Leaders must develop the ability to pick up the nuances of relationships and communication, noticing the norms developing within the group.

Our process for establishing group norms includes four basic elements:

1. Allow the group to air their previous experiences of groups

The aim is for each member of the group to talk and share something of his or her own experience. This in itself helps to set up the norm that everyone will talk in the group.

One way to do this is to have individuals record the best and worst things about groups they have been in. This is not a list of people and types of groups but a list of characteristics. Ask them to answer these questions:

> What have been the best things about small groups you have been in?

> What have been the worst things about small groups you have been in?

Collate everyone's comments on a large piece of paper, asking for clarification if it is needed. (Encourage those who have not been in a Bible study group before to think about sporting teams, work groups, school or university tutorials.) At this point you could allow the group to analyse the central issues and common themes arising from the discussion.

2. Help the participants to discuss their hopes and expectations for this particular group

This can be achieved by asking the group to complete one of the sets of questions below:

> From the leader in this group I expect…

> From the others in this group I expect…

> From myself in this group I expect…

Or

> By the end of the group I would like...
>
> I fear the group will not succeed in...
>
> During the life of the group I hope...
>
> I fear that during the group...[7]

Each person is to complete the set of questions personally and then share with the group. We get everyone to answer the first question before we move on to the second question, rather than one person sharing all of his or her comments at once. This allows the group to gain a sense of what everyone thinks on each question and it also models balanced participation. The group is enabled to develop a common purpose and an agreed method of achieving it. Some norms are developed in response to group interaction or an individual's reaction, for example: it is OK to disagree; or it is OK to cry in this group.

> **A basic rule is that something is always happening to the norms of a group, whether it be positive or negative, obvious or hidden.**

Most people will hope for acceptable things in a group. Occasionally, a person will have an expectation the group is unable to meet. For instance, someone might expect each member of the group to ring him every week. If this is unrealistic for your group, now is the time to address it. You could say 'I don't think the group will be able to achieve that. What do other members think?' or 'The aim of this group is to provide some level of support but I expect that we probably won't all form life-long friendships here. What do others think?' This means the issue can be defused early in the life of the group. If the person is still unhappy, you could gently suggest that this may not be the best group for him. It is better for the group as a whole if people with completely different expectations leave before the group actually begins.

3. Decide upon the norms and agree to adhere to them

Having completed stages one and two, the group then comes together to formalise how these hopes and expectations are going to be achieved. Develop a list of guidelines that people are willing to abide by. These need to be as few as possible and worded in the

---

7.   B. Dick, *Helping groups to be effective* (Chapel Hill: Interchange, 1991).

positive sense. You could say: 'We will **not** be late', but you could also frame it positively: 'We agree to arrive at 7.45 pm each week'. The difference might seem merely semantic, but it does create an affirmative impression. It is more helpful for the group to have a set of positive goals than a set of prohibitions.

Below is an example of a set of guidelines for one group we ran. The group spent some of the first week developing these guidelines and stuck to them over time:

> We expect people to turn up and be on time.
>
> We expect to be willing to discuss, ask questions, and let others finish.
>
> We expect that people will be willing to contribute.
>
> We expect people to tell others they are wrong, nicely.
>
> We expect that we will not cut in, or be arrogant.
>
> We expect to study the Bible regularly.

Notice that these are the sort of guidelines that most leaders want for their groups. Our experience has been that participants develop a set of guidelines almost identical to the ones we desire. The difference is that the group 'own' these and try to abide by them.

Such guidelines are often referred to as a 'contract', because the group is agreeing to commit itself to a set of behaviours. We avoid using this terminology with groups because some people find its legal overtones intimidating.

Each individual in the group must be willing to live with the guidelines. Sometimes a person will withdraw at this point. This has only happened to us once. After the group developed the guidelines a participant rang and said that although she thought the group would be fun, she did not want to be committed to turning up every week and so would withdraw. While it was disappointing for all of us, it meant there was less overall damage to the group than would have been created by her lack of attendance over time.

4. Hand out a record of these for the group members to keep

The final stage with group guidelines is to type them up to hand out the following week. A good technique is to type out the guidelines on the back of a list of group members' names and addresses so they will keep them.

Having worked through the process above, you are able to return to these guidelines if the group is not complying with them. The guidelines might need to be changed, or perhaps the group needs to be reminded of its commitment and challenged to adjust its behaviour.

This begins the process of establishing norms in your group. To further develop them the leader must be a careful role model. For instance, if you want people to be honest about the ups and downs of their relationship with God, then you have to initiate and model this. If you want people to feel comfortable in your house then you need to help them. For example, when we have a new group meeting in our home we give them a tour of the house. Here is the kitchen – coffee, tea, mugs, milk, biscuits. Help yourself. Here is the bathroom and the spare toilet paper. Handtowels are kept in this cupboard. Then we ask 'Who wants a drink?' The first person to say yes is asked if he or she would make drinks for everybody else. From then on it is assumed people help themselves and serve others.

As we have said, it is important to be aware that there are always norms developing in a group. Therefore as a leader it is best to take control and ensure these norms are ones which help you achieve your purpose.

When and where you meet

Your venue significantly influences group life, and will enhance or reduce the effectiveness of your time together. This section addresses some of the basic issues associated with choosing venue and time.

When you meet

Meeting times will vary from group to group, and arranging a time can be a difficult process. It is important to meet often enough to maintain continuity and build relationships. Groups that meet fortnightly often struggle to hold together, as a member who misses a meeting will not be seen for a month. On the other hand, some people find the demands of a weekly meeting overwhelming.

Similarly, it is important to meet at a time which is realistic in terms of energy levels, other commitments and individual demands. We were once members of a Friday night group and found we often could not attend because of family, social and other commitments. Others, however, found Friday night the perfect time to meet, as it was free from the pressure of work the following day.

You as a leader need to contemplate the different issues for yourself and potential members. Ensure you arrange a time which is convenient for yourself, as you will need to attend every meeting.

Choosing a venue

Make sure there is enough air and adequate lighting, and meet in a room that is not too large, not too small but just right. There needs to be enough air so that people are comfortable – not sitting in the path of a gale or sweltering in a stuffy box. Make sure there is enough light because people need to be able to see each other clearly and they need to be able to read their Bibles. Soft lighting looks nice, but it makes reading difficult and encourages drowsiness. Meet in a room of the right size so that people do not feel cramped or too distant from each other. Remember that different people have different definitions of personal space. Be aware of your personal preference as you will arrange the room in the way you think is comfortable, which may not be best for the group.

Seating arrangements

Eye contact, a smile or a nod can be used to give or withhold permission to speak in a group. Leaders can encourage or discourage participation in the group by giving people various meaningful 'looks'. The group leader can seat people in such a way as to make it easier for the less talkative, or in order to keep a dominating person quiet. Confrontation in a group is also affected by non-verbal communication. It is easier to disagree with someone when you are directly facing them, and you are less likely to disagree with someone right next to you. Therefore the seating arrangements will affect the way in which your group functions.

Consider the impact of each of these arrangements:

1.

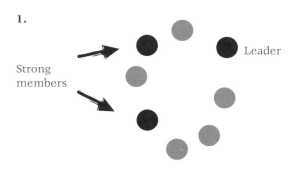

Strong members

Leader

The first situation is quite confrontational. The placing of the strong members in relation to the leader would encourage a style of conversation where the three dominate the interactions and everybody else is left watching the action.

2.

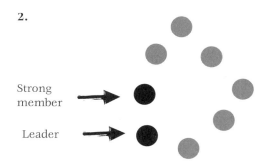

Strong member

Leader

The second example would enable the leader to avoid eye contact with the strong member and therefore discourage input from him or her. This could enable the quieter members of the group to participate more fully.

3.

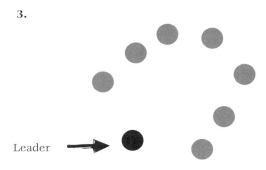

Leader

The third example has an elitist feel. The separation between the leader and the members implies some feeling of distance, which could be interpreted as keeping yourself apart from the group members.

Eye level

The height at which you sit will also affect a Bible study group. To enable everyone to feel equal, it is important that people are sitting on a similar level. We have seven nieces and nephews at our family Christmas dinners, and the children always sit at the smaller table on lower chairs. This says something about their status as well as their stature. Once a child is considered 'adult', he or she is allowed to sit at the big table. This status symbol is quite common in groups, and therefore it is important to offer seats on the same level to avoid the subtle denigration or elevation of some people. It is interesting to note that when the minister visits the group, he or she will be offered the biggest, most comfortable chair.

It is sometimes difficult to provide seating which puts everyone on an equal level, but it is worth the effort. Encourage people to sit at a similar height. The popular scene of lounging around on the floor may appear relaxed, but it causes major problems by making eye contact and discussion difficult.

Distractions

People can get easily distracted by such things as noise, activity and uncomfortable chairs. Try to meet in a place with as few distractions as possible. In other words, try to make it easy for people to concentrate on the business of studying the Bible. As an aside, always make sure your answering service is on if you have one, or leave your phone off the hook while the study is on. There is nothing more annoying than the leader always leaving the room to answer the phone.

Task and maintenance functions

Let us tell you the story of a group. The group is fictitious, but we are sure you will recognise the type of situation.

> A group was formed to run a conference. The group had a life of about a year. All the members thoroughly supported the conference and its aims. The leader, Isabelle, had lots of experience in leading conference groups and was very efficient. The other members were all committed Christians, who, although inexperienced, were each keen to help organise an excellent conference.
>
> The members' enthusiasm made the group appear to function well at its first meeting. After the initial introductions the group immediately got down to work. Isabelle explained the purpose of the conference and began to delegate tasks. The group members, who had little experience, were surprised at the brusqueness of the beginning but attributed this to their ignorance of conference organisation. The meeting finished in prayer and people went home.
>
> The group continued to meet regularly, although not everyone attended each meeting. This was partly due to some people feeling dominated by Isabelle and unable to contribute. Some people began to feel they were simply functionaries to help Isabelle do her job. Isabelle found this frustrating and pushed the group harder to get through the work. She encouraged the group to remain task-focused. She said there was no need for chatting or finding out about how people were going, because the group was formed to do a job and not to have nice talks with each other.

As the conference drew nearer, attendance at meetings dropped further, and the workload on individuals increased. When challenged about why they did not attend, some people said the group wasn't much fun. They said they had expected to be able to get to know the others as well as do the job. Others said they did not feel their contribution was appreciated. Isabelle's response was that people lacked commitment and maturity. People were offended, and more withdrew.

By the time the conference began, some tasks were not completed and a number of things went wrong. People felt disappointed, frustrated and even embarrassed because the conference was not what they had hoped for. Isabelle felt betrayed and let down. By the end of the conference, the committee members were glad to go home and a number decided never to participate in that sort of group again. Most of the committee did not see each other after it was all over.

 How do you assess what happened in this group? It obviously was not an effective group, although the conference happened almost to plan. Did you pick up any indicators of problems before they arose?

Every group, whether it is a Bible study group or conference committee or parish council, has task functions and maintenance functions. An effective group needs an appropriate balance of the two.

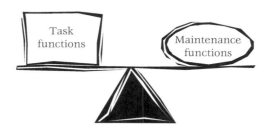

Task functions are the activities of the leader and the members which enable the group to achieve its stated purpose. In Isabelle's group, the task was the organisation of the conference.

The first issue to be addressed in a group is 'What is the purpose?' or 'Why do we meet?' In a Bible study group the easy answer to this is: to study the Bible. But surely the purpose of a Bible study group is much more than that. It must be clearly understood that the purpose of a Bible study group is to enable people to develop their relationship with God, through studying the Bible together. Studying the Bible is therefore a means to an end, rather than the end in itself.

Maintenance functions are the activities which the leaders and the members perform to enable the relationship side of the group to develop. They are necessary to help the group function as a group.

For example, our experience when we are working hard on a particular project is that we need to be very particular about exercise and diet. While it may initially seem that these can be sacrificed in order to get on with the job, we have learned that eating well and having proper exercise actually enable us to achieve more. Proper maintenance is essential for completing the task. Clearly, it would be absurd if we only had maintenance and never got on with the task. We need a proper balance between the two.

While Isabelle's group had good task functions initially, it is clear that the maintenance functions were inadequate. It is also clear the group members wanted to achieve their goal of running the conference but this was sabotaged by the lack of relationship. After the initial introductions, there was never any mention of what people did in the rest of their lives. Apparently, Isabelle assumed that the only interesting thing about these people was their function on this committee. As the relationships deteriorated the attendance started to wane. At this point, the lack of maintenance started to hinder the achievement of the task.

Fun is a very important maintenance function. As the tension in meetings rose, there was no helpful way for people to relieve tension. Even though people tried to concentrate on the issues all the time, it simply was not possible. Fun in the group was curtailed by Isabelle because she considered it 'a waste of time'. However, it would have enabled the group to get on with the task.

In any group, no matter what the purpose, both task and maintenance functions are indispensable. The maintenance functions enable the group to achieve the task more easily. If Isabelle had been prepared to spend more time on developing relationships within the group, and allowed some fun into the group time, then the task may have been achieved more effectively. As it was, there was no relationship and therefore no commitment to either the group or the task.

Different behaviours make up the two types of functions.

1. Task behaviours:
    information and opinion giving;
    information and opinion seeking;
    direction and role defining;
    summarising;
    energising;
    comprehension checking;
    diagnosing.

2. Maintenance behaviours:
    encouraging participation;
    facilitating communication;
    relieving tension;
    observing process;
    solving interpersonal problems;
    supporting and praising;
    expressing feelings;
    following;
    compromising;
    harmonising;
    setting standards.

These are not the only behaviours for each of these categories, simply some of the more common ones. Notice these behaviours are not restricted to the designated leader. They can be carried out by members of the group as well.

1. Task behaviours

✦ **Information and opinion giving**
    People help the group to achieve the task by being open about the information they possess, and sharing facts, ideas and feelings among the group.

✦ **Information and opinion seeking**
    People help the group achieve the task by inquiring of others about their information, facts, feelings and views.

✦ **Direction and role defining**
    People help the group achieve its task by asking questions and offering opinions about the direction of the group, and the purpose of individual members within it. They assign tasks and responsibilities.

✦ **Summarising**
People offer summary statements of discussions and arguments, which enable the group to see where it has been and where it is going.

✦ **Energising**
The person with this role reinvigorates the group if they are flagging. He or she encourages the group to work hard at the task.

✦ **Comprehension checking**
People ask questions which ensure that the whole group has understood what was said and what it meant.

✦ **Diagnosing**
People offer opinions about the difficulties the group might be experiencing and how they might be solved. They will be observing and reporting back to the group any blockages or interventions needed.

2. Maintenance behaviours

✦ **Encouraging participation**
People help develop interpersonal relationships by actively seeking participation from other members.

✦ **Facilitating communication**
People help to maintain the functioning of the group by ensuring that all have the opportunity to speak, and those who are dominating are helped to recognise the nature of their participation.

✦ **Relieving tension**
This person is commonly known as the Joker. He or she helps the group to grow together personally by providing opportunities to laugh. While the Joker can get out of control, he or she serves a useful function since the common experience of a joke is relationship building.

✦ **Observing relationships**
People observe the way group members relate and report back those observations to others.

✦ **Solving interpersonal problems**
To help the group grow relationally, people offer suggestions regarding difficult encounters with others in the group. They reduce tension by clarifying differences and reconciling disagreements.

✦ **Supporting and praising**
   People help the group by offering support and praise wherever it is due.

✦ **Expressing feelings**
   People build the relational side of the group by offering and asking for people's feelings on a matter. Even in a task-focused group, this is an important role.

✦ **Following**
   People enable the group to function by being willing to accept leadership and participate as needed.

✦ **Setting standards**
   People both demonstrate and express the type of behaviour acceptable in this group, and encourage others to work to that standard.

It is important that all the functions are performed as required in a group. The leader needs to make sure this happens. This does not necessarily mean doing everything yourself, but ensuring that somebody does.

You may be wondering how Bible study group leaders can manage all these functions. This huge list of behaviours can be overwhelming. Think in terms of what is manageable. If reading this list has made you aware of weaknesses in your leadership, work on developing those areas. This will take time and effort. Simply being aware of an area of weakness helps, but praying about it and acting deliberately to change is also important.

Some groups have two leaders, which can work well. In co-leadership situations there are potentially four ways of dealing with all the requirements:

1.   Leave it all up to whoever is leading on a particular night. This places an enormous burden on one person, and could leave the group confused as to what the other leader is doing on his or her 'night off'.

2.   Make the person leading the Bible study responsible for the task functions and the co-leader responsible for the maintenance functions. An advantage is that the person leading the Bible study can focus better, but a disadvantage is that forgetting the maintenance functions during a Bible study could lead to an intellectual approach.

3. Both leaders might 'play it by ear' and do whatever they think needs doing at the time. This has the advantage of being more natural, but could mean that important functions are missed because neither of the leaders notice. This can also create difficulties if the leaders disagree about the type of intervention needed in the group.

4. Each person does what doesn't come naturally to him or her. Yes, that's right – what doesn't come naturally! If one person is more task-focused by nature, he or she is responsible for the maintenance functions in this Bible study – and vice versa. This has the advantage of ensuring that both leaders have to think hard about their responsibilities, and are developing skills as they learn more. Consequently, they will be more rounded leaders when they need to function alone.

Are there things you need to change in order to help your group function better? Use the questionnaire on the following pages to reflect on your leadership.

Work through the list of task/maintenance behaviours and note the ones which you regard as personal weaknesses. Choose one or two of these, and record possible ways to strengthen your leadership behaviour.

Starting the group well

Beginning well sets the tone for the rest of the year, as people get to know each other. What can leaders do to help people to get to know each other?

Early in the group's life, it is important to have activities that encourage people to talk about themselves. This is crucial for developing trust, respect, clear and open communication, cohesion and balanced participation. The quality of the foundations laid will influence the ongoing effectiveness of the group.

It is difficult to find exercises that work and do not make people feel embarrassed. Over the years we have collected the following activities. You will need to assess whether they will work for your group within the available time. Some of them are short and snappy while others take longer but are more informative. Use a mixture for variety and fun. To establish a group well, we would do one of these each week or fortnight for four to six weeks.

Task/maintenance questionnaire[8]

Score 5 if the statement is always true
Score 4 if the statement is usually true
Score 3 if the statement is frequently true
Score 2 if the statement is occasionally true
Score 1 if the statement is rarely true
Score 0 if the statement is never true

1. I ensure the group correctly understands and appropriately applies the Bible. ....

2. I listen and give feedback, demonstrating understanding, empathy and concern. ....

3. I provide clear instructions and ensure people know what they need to do. ....

4. I challenge others to grow and develop in their Christian faith. ....

5. I initiate prayer as a regular component of group time. ....

6. I encourage balanced participation by drawing some out and limiting others. ....

7. I inject humour into and encourage fun in group sessions. ....

8. I ensure the group starts and finishes promptly, with time used effectively. ....

9. I take risks, and encourage others to do the same by being trustworthy. ....

10. I set clear and realistic goals and objectives. ....

11. I notice tension and conflict, and act to help resolve it. ....

12. I measure and assess the group's progress towards its goal. ....

13. I notice the participation, feelings, and interpersonal interactions of group members. ....

14. I help people be relaxed and at ease. ....

15. I plan and implement strategies to fulfil the group's goals. ....

16. I initiate social interaction and build interpersonal relationships. ....

17. I maintain discipline and structure within the Bible study. ....

18. I communicate respect by valuing individual contributions. ....

19. I ask questions to clarify and promote understanding. ....

20. I discern the underlying thoughts and feelings in other people's comments and questions. ....

---

8. This questionnaire was developed with the assistance of participants in the Small Group Leadership course conducted at Moore Theological College in 1997.

Scoring for task/maintenance questionnaire

1. Total your score for all questions. The difference between this score and 100 indicates the potential for growth in your overall leadership.

    100 -

    Total score: _____

Potential for growth as a leader:

2. Add your scores for task behaviours and maintenance behaviours to determine the relative strengths of each.

Task behaviours	
Question	Score
1	
3	
4	
5	
8	
10	
12	
15	
17	
19	
Total Task	

Maintenance behaviours	
Question	Score
2	
6	
7	
9	
11	
13	
14	
16	
18	
20	
Total Maintenance	

3. Using the score for total task and total maintenance, plot your position on this grid. The goal is to move towards the top right hand corner of the grid, reflecting strong scores in both task focused and maintenance focused behaviours.

Task focused behaviours

50
40
30
20
10

0   10   20   30   40   50

Maintenance focused behaviours

Each of these activities can be adjusted to your group. They work on the assumption that the leader is asking probing questions in response to people's answers. They are best when they move quickly instead of getting bogged down in detail. The essential requirement is that they be fun for the people involved.

Remember, these activities are to help the group function more effectively so it can get on with the job of studying the Bible. They are not meant to be used as the single focus for a Bible study session.

✦   **Five favourite things**

Ask people to think of five things they would take with them if they were to spend a day alone. This activity helps you to work out what interests another person and what is important to them. Give the group a couple of minutes to work out what they would take, and then ask them to share their answers around the group.

✦   **Who's who**

Ask each person to write a list of five obscure or unknown things about him/herself on a piece of paper and then scrunch it up and throw it into the middle of the group. When everyone has finished, ask each person to get a piece of paper from the middle of the circle and read the list to the rest of the group.

As each one is read, the rest of the group has to guess who the person is. Score two points for guessing correctly and minus one for a wrong guess. At the end, the person with the most points gets a prize. It is best if you choose a prize that can be shared around the group, such as a bag of lollies.

✦   **Monday morning**

Go around the group asking each person what is the first thing he or she does on a Monday, and why.

✦   **Holiday dreaming**

Ask the group to plan their ultimate holiday, assuming they have plenty of money and time. Where would they go? Who would they go with? How would they get there? What would they take? Have each person share around the group.

✦   **Friendship factors**

This can get a bit deep, so do not do it too early in the life of the group. Ask people to describe three things they value in a friendship.

✦ Have you ever?

This is a game some people would be familiar with from school or youth group. It is good fun, especially if it moves quickly.

Form all the chairs into a circle with one chair less than the number of people in the group. The leader stands in the centre of the circle, and the group members sit on the chairs. The leader asks a question beginning with the words 'Have you ever...?' All the members of the group who answer 'yes' to the question must change chairs. They are not allowed to move to the chairs on either side of the ones they are on. The object is for the person asking the question to get a seat while the others are moving. Whoever is left standing then has to ask the next question.

The questions can be trivial or deep, with the only proviso being that the person asking the question must be able to answer 'yes' to it. This means inappropriate questions are not asked.

Sample questions:

Have you ever used someone else's toothbrush?

Have you ever been hang-gliding?

Have you ever seen a whale?

Have you ever been disappointed with God?

... and anything else the group can think of.

✦ Sibling rivalry

This exercise works best with a group of more than ten. Ask people to join with others who have the same position in the family as themselves. There should be four groups: oldest, youngest, middle child and only child. Then ask each group to present to the rest of the group the good things and bad things about being in that position in the family.

✦ Feelings marketplace

This activity requires a set of Feelings Marketplace cards, available from the Camping Association of Victoria. It is a collection of about 60 cards with a single emotion written on each one.

Each person is handed four or five cards and the group is given a question to answer: How do you feel about small groups? Describe your growing up. Tell us what work is like. Tell us about your best and worst holidays.

The group is then given the chance to barter their cards so they can collect words that accurately reflect their answer to the question.

Then each person answers the question using the cards they ended up with. We usually encourage people to place the cards in front of themselves as they speak.

✦   **Photo language**

This activity requires a set of Photo Language cards, produced by the Catholic Education Office in Sydney. These cards are a collection of photos which people use to illustrate their response to a question. For instance, ask people to choose a photo which expresses their reaction to church. Then ask them to explain why they chose that particular photo.

✦   **Lifelines**

This activity requires a piece of paper and a pen for each person. Ask each person to map a time line of his or her life, which shows the ups and downs over time. Everyone then explains their time line to the group. This takes some time, so make sure you do not feel rushed when doing it. We have sometimes taken two weeks to hear everyone's story. While this may seem like a huge investment of time, we have found this activity extremely helpful for assisting a group to appreciate each other.

✦   **Personal shield**

This exercise requires paper and enough felt pens for each person to be able to have a few different colours.

Ask the group to draw a shield on their paper – as big as they can make it. You will need to demonstrate what it looks like.

Then ask them to divide it into quarters and draw something different on each quadrant, for example:

Quadrant 1: A favourite place

Quadrant 2: A significant person

Quadrant 3: Where you grew up

Quadrant 4: A favourite thing

Vary the questions according to what you wish the group to discuss. Have each person explain his or her personal shield to the rest of the group.

✦ Prouds and sorries

This is also an activity for later in the group's life, since it requires quite a high level of self-disclosure. Have each person complete the sentences:

> I am proud that...

> I am sorry that...

We usually get all the group to share their 'proud' answer before their 'sorry'.

✦ Autograph scavenger hunt

This activity requires a bit of preparation. Before the group meets, the leader needs to create a scavenger hunt list similar to one of those shown below. The categories need to be appropriate for the group.

The object is to get a signature in every space and the first person with a full sheet wins.

The person whose birthday is closest to yours	
Someone who dislikes a food you also dislike	
Someone who has received a love poem	
Someone who has been a Christian more than three years	
Someone who has been outside Australia	
Someone who has made a piece of furniture	
Someone who likes the same sort of car as you	
Someone who has been a Christian less than three years	
Someone who has more than one brother or sister	
Someone who has seen at least two movies you have seen	
Someone who has done some exercise	

Find someone who has:				
sailed on a yacht	crossed the equator	been in mud up to his or her waist	used a glass cutter	dived into a pool and lost his or her swimmers
ridden on a steam train	played an instrument in front of an audience	seen an iceberg	been to a black tie function	had a blind date
been to seven countries	milked a cow or goat	found more than $50	gone to sleep during a lecture	made a piece of furniture
swallowed a raw egg	worn braces	seen a koala in the wild	had a wart removed	given blood
walked on stilts	watched three videos in a row	written a 'letter to the editor'	eaten raw oysters	broken a record
cried because of a movie or song	written a poem	had heat exhaustion	coloured his or her hair	been to a chiropractor
hitchhiked	owned more than one cat at a time	stayed out all night	raised silk worms	ridden in a shopping trolley
been knocked out	held a snake in his or her hands	painted a house	had acupuncture	had something published

Once you have a winner, ask the group to sit down again and find out who signed which space and why. This can be light-hearted and fun, and does not need to take long.

✦ **Presenting my partner**

You need paper and a pen for each person.

Direct the members of the group to pair up with someone they do not know and draw that person while discussing some questions. While drawing, do not raise your pen from the paper or look at the page. (This removes people's concerns about their drawing ability.)

People then show their drawings to the rest of the group and explain their partners' answers to the questions.

The questions might include: What the other person enjoys, the most significant thing he or she has done, or an issue he or she feels passionately about.

The object is to make the group laugh while finding out more about the individuals.

✦ **Testimonies**

Explaining how you became a Christian or describing your spiritual journey is a great way to get to know others in your group.

✦ **Quaker questions**

This is an activity we have used many times. We are not sure why it is called 'Quaker questions', but we do know it works! It is a series of questions of increasing depth and self-disclosure.

Describe the place you lived at age ten.

Describe your funniest memory.

Describe your first thoughts about God.

Describe your spiritual journey over recent years.

Describe where you expect your spiritual journey to go in the next two years.

Ask everyone to jot down some notes to help them answer the questions and then have each person share his or her responses. We find it helpful to have everyone comment on the first question before progressing to the next. We continue this way for every statement.

✦ **Kaleidoscopic Karen**

We call this game Kaleidoscopic Karen, because Raucous Rod seemed inappropriate! The object is to help people remember other people's names.

Go around the group introducing yourself with an adjective that starts with the same letter as your name. The adjective can also be descriptive of yourself: Sensible Susan or Delirious Danny. At the end, ask if anybody can remember everybody's name and test them out. This is a good activity at the second or third meeting of a group, where people feel they should remember other's names, but cannot actually do it.

✦ **My name and how I got it**

Ask each person to tell the group his or her full name and how he or she got it. This is a variation of 'Kaleidoscopic Karen' which works in a similar way. We often use one, and then use the other at the next meeting.

✦ **See me mad...**

Hand out a sheet with a list of sentence beginnings, and ask people to complete the sentences. Below is one we have used, but you could use anything you like. Share the answers around the group after people have finished writing.

Anyone will work hard if...

People who run things should...

Nothing is so frustrating as...

I take pride in...

If you want to see me get mad...

A rewarding job is one that...

A mature Christian is...

✦ **My house history**

Everyone draws two or three houses they have lived in and explains their experience of these places. Ask such things as: Where was the house? Who else lived there? What was it like for you?

✦ **Mapping my life**

Ask each participant to draw a freehand map of Australia and to mark various places. The places might include where you grew up, where you went on holidays, your favourite place in Australia, where you would like to go. You might include a place that indicates where you are spiritually, for example the desert: dry, lifeless, waiting for rain; or the city: bustling, excited. This is a particularly Australian activity but, with obvious modifications, it could be used in any country.

Have each person explain his or her map to the rest of the group.

✦ **Oh to be an aardvark**

Give everyone about a minute to choose the animal they would be if they could be. Then tell the group and explain why.

✦ **A representative remnant**

This activity is best when the group is away from the normal environment, for instance on a weekend away together. Give the group fifteen minutes to find something in the area that represents some aspect of their group or personal life. As the leader you need to decide what aspect you want them to depict. It could include:

> How are you spiritually?

> How do you think the group is going?

> What is your life like at the moment?

Once they have decided on an object, ask each person to explain why he or she chose it. For instance, one person may choose an empty soft drink can, to indicate that she is feeling spiritually dry; another might choose a flower bud, to show that he is expecting future growth.

✦ **Moving movies**

Ask each participant to tell the rest of the group about a movie or a book that had an impact on him or her, and why it did.

Finishing well

Ending well allows people the freedom to move on without feelings of guilt or regret. What can you do to end a group well? The mourning process has the potential to be a celebratory conclusion or a depressing disintegration. Done well, the mourning can help people to grieve the loss of their group and look forward to the future. The single most significant responsibility of the leader at this point is to explain to the group what is happening and what might happen in the future. This could be explained using the phases of group life or a shortened version of it, and giving people permission to grieve the loss involved. The activities used here need to be carefully selected, taking into account the nature of the group.

To understand the nature of mourning, we need to look at the needs of the members. Each group will be different, but there are likely to be some common requirements of most groups. The group's needs fall into two categories: security and significance. Their need for security and significance is much like that of a child leaving home. They need to know they are valued and loved, while also knowing it is safe to leave and relationships will cope with the change. The fear of ruining important relationships will often keep a teenager at home. The same fear can also keep people in a group.

The need for security demands two things from the leader. The group members need to know what is going to happen and when, and they need to know that relationships will finish in a way that allows ends and new beginnings. They must know a final date for closure and whether the group will continue next year or not. They also need to know that they won't be deserted by these people. There are other ways you can meet the group's need for security at the end, but we have found these to be the most important.

'Significance' describes the individual's need to feel he or she has contributed to making this group function well. The members of the group need to know they have mattered to each other and are valued. They also need to hear what the group meant to each person. In terms of the group as a whole, there needs to be some acknowledgment of achievement.

Given these needs, there are two things that are important in closing a group. **The first is a time of reflection which includes sharing among the group.** With a bit of imagination, many of the 'starting well' activities can be modified for finishing well. Other exercises we have used include:

✦ Attach a big piece of paper to each person's back and hand out pens to every participant. Then ask group members to go around and write on each piece of paper what that person meant to them or contributed to the group.

✦ Ask the participants to make a list of the things that have been important to them during the course of the group and to share these. Having discussed these things, talk about the things each person is looking forward to doing next year.

✦ The group could 'mind map' all the things they have learned over the year, to develop the idea that they actually achieved something. A mind map involves doing a diagram of all the topics covered and the things remembered.

To draw a mind map, have the group identify the central topic, and then draw branches from the centre for each major sub-topic. The group then adds extensions to these branches to indicate significant ideas within that sub-topic. (An example is shown on the next page.)

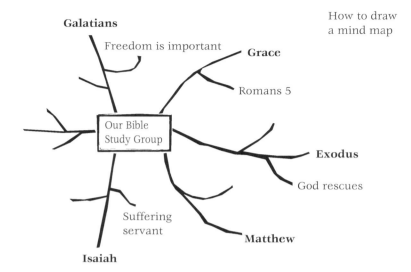

How to draw
a mind map

The second important activity for a group at this stage of their life is a celebration. This is almost in the form of a wake. There is sadness at the loss, but a celebration of the life. In our experience the best celebrations always involve food. They are a time to be silly and laugh as well as eat together and pray for each other.

Starting well and finishing well always involve thought and planning. With the right sort of input, the leader can set the tone of the group and celebrate the group's life.

A note about finishing for leaders: We commented earlier that leaders need to exercise greater care and plan more deliberately as a group enters its final stages. This means that a leader will work particularly hard at the beginning and end of a group's life, while the group itself will exercise greater initiative during the middle period of a group. This can be pictured in the following way:

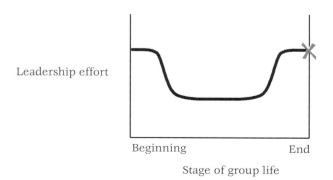

The significance of the X in the diagram is that leaders finish the group having made a lot of effort in the final few weeks. This often leaves us feeling quite disappointed the following week when the Bible study group would normally meet. Our response to this has been to have our own celebratory dinner at the time we would usually have been meeting with the group.

While it is encouraging when a group goes well, there are a number of dangers which leaders should try to avoid. First, it is often the case that group members want to prolong the life of the group. While this sounds good it is actually detrimental, as it hinders people from moving on. It also increases the feeling of loss and regret when the group meets again and the experience is not really the same as before.

Secondly, members from a particularly positive group can become annoying when they enter another group and continually draw comparisons with their last group. This prevents them from fully becoming part of their new group and can create conflict. We have seen a situation where a member of the new group has suggested that the new member might like to return to where he or she came from if it was so good. This behaviour causes anxiety all round, and could have been avoided if the new member had been warned in advance. We remind people that they will be comparing their new group to one that has been going for a year or two. We remind them of what the group was like when it first started, and we encourage them to be patient and work hard at helping their new group develop.

Intervening when things go wrong

We hope that things always go well in your groups, but it is helpful to know how to intervene when things go wrong. As leader, you intervene in the activities of the group in order to bring about a desired outcome. The image we find most helpful when considering leader interventions is the image of 'a fork in the road'. The fork represents a point in a group's life which the leader must be able to recognise and respond to. It is a decision point where the group could proceed in a variety of ways. The role of the leader is to guide the group by whatever intervention is chosen, so that the group continues on its journey.

There are six situations in the life of a group when the group leader should intervene:

1. when the group is in danger of misinterpreting or misapplying a passage of Scripture;

2. when the leader observes that the group is bogged down;

3. when the group begins to deal with an issue but then avoids it;

4. when members are unable to make the connections that would enable them to progress further on their task;

5. when group members have not noticed progress which has been made, which would provide insight and understanding if they did notice it.

6. when a no-go area develops or when members are unable to resolve conflict.[9]

The effective group leader is like a good physician. Just about anyone can tell that a person is sick, but the physician can identify the disease and prescribe the necessary remedy. There are some illnesses which are not obvious until they reach an advanced stage, at which point they are beyond treatment. If recognised and treated early they can be cured. It is this ability to perceive early warning signs which is the real skill of the good physician. Likewise, an effective group leader can suggest remedies for obvious problems and also detect and provide preventive remedies for potential or developing problems. In order to do this it is necessary to have a framework which moves you beyond the obvious.

The issue of intervention in a group's learning involves the leader in the full gambit of group dynamics issues. The ability to identify, analyse and respond to the needs of the group is essential. Leaders are required to 'read' the group as it changes.

There are three models which we find particularly helpful when considering leadership interventions.

1. Stages of group development

The group development model discussed previously identified five stages: forming, norming, storming, performing and mourning. It allows you to consider where the group is at developmentally and therefore respond according to the stage of growth.

9. Adapted from R. Boyd, 'An approach to facilitating personal transformations in small groups' *Small group research*, Vol 21 No 4, (Nov 1990), 522–537.

2. 'Force field' analysis

This can be used to identify elements within a group which either facilitate or restrain change for an individual or the group.

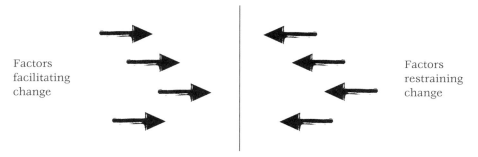

Factors facilitating change

Factors restraining change

In order to facilitate change, you must identify and respond to both sets of factors in a way that promotes the growth of the group. In particular, it is helpful to work at reducing the restraining forces in order to help change happen. It is a bit like driving a car. You can either accelerate harder or release the handbrake. Both will cause some movement, but releasing the brake is more helpful.

This model suggests the leader can help the group most effectively by addressing some of the issues holding back the group. For example, you might notice that Anne sometimes seems annoyed with others in the group. The factors facilitating change include her enthusiasm and commitment to the group, the challenge and encouragement of others in the group, the work of the Holy Spirit in her life, and so on. The factors restraining growth include busyness and tiredness, lack of understanding, and poor communication skills. On reflection, you decide her tiredness on some evenings means she is more likely to get annoyed with others in the group.

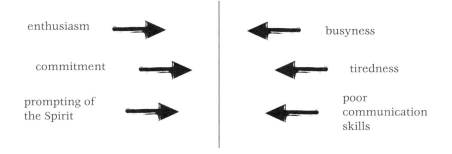

enthusiasm

commitment

prompting of the Spirit

busyness

tiredness

poor communication skills

Having identified this issue, the leader now has to decide what type of intervention would be most helpful. This is where the third model comes in.

3. The intervention cube[10]

We like this model as it recognises that the leader can deal with what the group is thinking, feeling or doing, and do so at the level of individual, subgroup or whole group, with multiple variations and combinations of these elements.

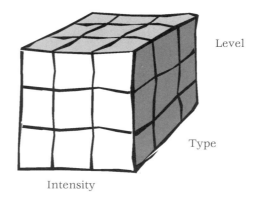

The intervention cube sees the leader as having options in regard to the **level**, **type** and **intensity** of interventions.

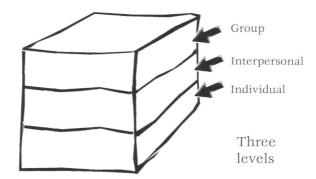

There are three **levels** within a group at which a facilitator can intervene. These are the individual, interpersonal and whole group level. You might talk specifically to Anne, or to a few members of the group, or to the whole group. This is the level of intervention.

---

10. A.Cohen and R. Smith, *The critical incident in group growth* (La Jolla: University Associates, 1976).

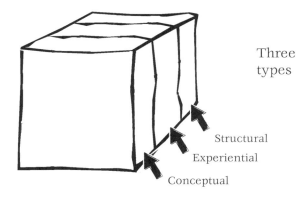

Three
types

Structural

Experiential

Conceptual

The three **types** of intervention are the conceptual (planned or spontaneous theoretical input), the experiential (dealing with the current group experience) and the structural. A spontaneous conceptual intervention would be to make some comments about work and busyness, while a planned conceptual intervention may be a series of studies looking at the fruit of the Spirit in the believer's life. An experiential intervention would involve discussing how the group was functioning and particularly how people felt about Anne's annoyed behaviour. A structural intervention could involve asking Anne to leave the group or moving the group meeting to a time at which Anne was less tired.

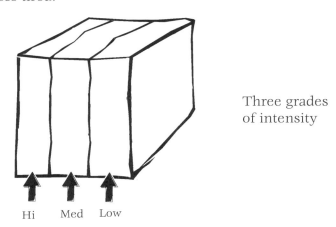

Three grades
of intensity

Hi   Med   Low

The intended **intensity** of interventions can range through high, medium or low. Intensity of intervention is a variable based on the leader's use of direction and authority. The higher the intensity, the more the leader directs and dictates to the group. The lower the intensity, the more the leader allows the group to have autonomy and self control. The intensity of the intervention involves deciding how much of an issue to make of the situation. Do you read Anne the riot act or have a quiet chat with her over supper? Do you confront her or gently correct her? Do you act in a way that is obviously directed at Anne or do you deal with it subtly so that nobody notices?

Our general approach with interventions is to start softly and increase the intensity as needed. If this was the first time this issue had arisen in the group, we would probably chat to Anne over supper. If however, it seemed to be a pattern for a number of group members, we would deal with it at the group level by planning some studies which raised the issues of work, tiredness and relationships. Usually, we restrict experiential and structural interventions to situations where there is a need for immediate damage control to maintain the wellbeing of the group.

A final note on intervening in the group. When you do it, remember you are not a passive agent in a mechanistic process, but an individual who interacts with other people. Therefore, you must be aware that your actions are not neutral and detached, but rather the actions of someone enmeshed in the situation and in relationship with the others. As the leader, do not assume your perspective is the same as the group's, or that it is necessarily correct.

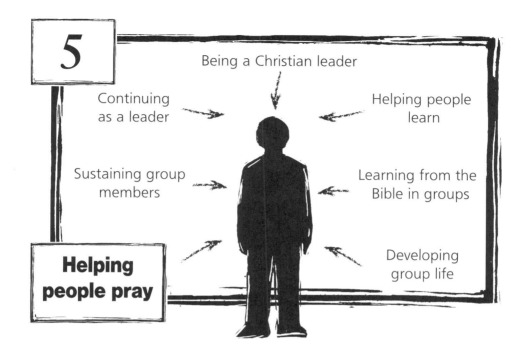

5

Being a Christian leader

Continuing as a leader

Helping people learn

Sustaining group members

Learning from the Bible in groups

Helping people pray

Developing group life

Prayer is often emphasised in theory in Bible study groups, yet neglected in practice. We know of groups which run out of time and have only a perfunctory prayer to open and close the meeting; of others which never move beyond the mundane and superficial; and of still others where only one or two people pray, while everyone else remains silent.

This is a problem. Our aim as Bible study group leaders is to help people grow in their relationship with Christ. This is more than simply acquiring head knowledge about the Bible or being socialised to behave in a way that is acceptable to a particular Christian sub-culture. It means helping people increase their knowledge of Scripture, grow stronger in their love for Jesus, grow more certain in their hope and stronger in their faith. It means helping people relate to God on his terms, and that means helping people pray, both individually and corporately. Prayer is our response to God, an expression of our love for him and our dependence upon him.

Praying aloud is a major component of Christian fellowship. We encourage each other and bring our common concerns to God. We aim to help everyone participate and make prayer an important part of our group life. Personal prayer is a major part of a vital relationship with God and something which we strive to nourish in individuals.

As leaders of Bible study groups, our role in helping people pray is threefold. We model a mature prayer life, we teach people how to pray, and we encourage them in actually doing it.

Modelling

Consider your own prayer life. What attitude do you communicate in your group? Are you a prayer giant, a prayer pygmy, or something else?

A number of years ago, Rod visited a friend who was recovering from surgery on his knee after a soccer mishap. As Rod arrived, Peter limped down the driveway to greet him, accompanied by his young son who was learning to walk. Both father and son were limping as they walked: Peter because of the ongoing pain in his knee, and Timothy because that was the way his Dad walked.

The example of others is crucial as we learn and develop. As we commented in Chapter 1: 'Being a Christian leader', people copy what they see you do more than what you say. Your attitudes and actions will be imitated by those in your group, whether you like it or not. Your practice is a model that others imitate. Therefore you need to deliberately set an example of genuine prayerfulness and self-disclosure which helps others understand what it means to pray in a group. This is hard work, but it is crucial if people are going to have an example worth copying. As a starting point, we recommend you consider your own prayer life and the sort of example you provide for those in your group.

ACTS as a model

One simple outline for a prayer life is provided by the acronym *ACTS.*

Adoration
Confession
Thanksgiving
Supplication

A is for adoration, encouraging us to respond to God as he is revealed in Scripture. **C** is for confession, focusing on our relationship with God and our need for forgiveness. **T** is for thanksgiving, allowing us to recall the abundant blessings we have received in Christ, and **S** is for supplication, providing the opportunity to bring all our needs before God.

You can use this model in your personal prayers, and adapt it for group use. **Adoration** may involve praying as some of the psalmists do, focusing on an aspect of God's character such as his faithfulness or his mighty acts. **Confession** involves assessing our lives from God's point of view, and saying sorry for the shortcomings we see. The group may do this as silent prayer, or through writing, or aloud in response to a passage which describes God's holiness or his purposes for his people. It is encouraging for a group to pray aloud when **thanking** God, identifying all the good things he has done for us, especially answered prayers. **Supplication** involves relying upon God's care for us by asking him for our needs and concerns. It is good to include prayers for things outside the group, such as missionaries and world issues, as well as individual needs.

Teaching people how

Expecting people to begin praying in a group without assistance is unrealistic. Some people feel intimidated, others embarrassed, others ignorant, and others unworthy. Some feel their concerns are irrelevant, others think they can't because they don't know all the right words, and others are simply scared of speaking aloud in a group. Whatever the reason, we can assume that we need to teach people how to pray. This is especially true for a new group with young Christians in it, but it is a useful assumption whenever you lead a group.

The benefit of assuming that you need to teach the group is that it places everyone on an equal footing, and it establishes a shared understanding of prayer within the group. This helps create a reasonable experience of prayer within the group and ensures younger Christians are not intimidated by the way others seem so confident in the group prayer time. For older Christians it provides an opportunity to begin praying without the embarrassment and stress of doing it for the first time in a new group. There will sometimes be people who do not want to pray out loud in a group and it is important to respect this, but helping them move to the point where they usually will pray is beneficial. We do not expect every person to pray at every meeting, but we do hope that everyone will usually participate.

A simple process

When beginning a new group, we aim to teach people how to pray over the first couple of months of the group's life (6–12 meetings, depending on how it goes). The object is to move slowly and not pressure anyone. Help people develop an understanding of what to pray, and build their confidence to do it in the group as the weeks progress. We use a simple process, which you can modify as needed.

The first principle is to establish a common goal regarding the prayer life of the group. If this was not decided when the group originally discussed expectations, it will be necessary to reach agreement now. What does the group want its prayer life to be like? It is important to establish a goal consistent with the overall purpose of understanding Scripture and spiritual growth. It may be necessary for the leader to give input and direction if the group is reluctant to commit to a suitable goal.

The second principle is to begin by taking small steps. We start with a very simple sentence completion activity, and build up over a few weeks making each successive step a little more complicated. People develop confidence as they successfully complete a series of simple prayers. Start slowly, providing clear guidelines and keeping things simple. Do not expect people to pray confidently from the very beginning. Laying the foundations well enables greater spontaneity later in the life of the group.

This process has various modifications, but this is the basic idea: Ask people to write their prayers down, and then have them read their own or someone else's prayer out loud. Extend the scope of the prayer week by week. In the first week we ask people to write on a piece of paper:

> Dear God, I thank you that…

and then write an end to the sentence in their own words. This enables everyone to participate without needing fancy words or long sentences. The pages are then swapped among people and the completed sentence is read aloud by another person. The reason for this is that most people are happy to read a short sentence aloud, especially when someone else has written it. This means everyone in the group speaks during the prayer time, and it establishes a pattern of participation and simplicity. The following week, the same activity is repeated, but people read their own sentences. Writing in advance gives people security, while reading their own sentences means they get used to formulating their own prayers.

In the third week, we add an extra element to the activity. We ask people to complete the following:

Dear God, I thank you that...

and I ask that...

Everyone then swaps so they read someone else's prayer. In week four we repeat week three, but we ask people to read their own prayers.

After four weeks, we usually find people are keen to have a longer prayer, so we prepare a simple outline which is handed out for people to complete. We ask people to keep their prayers simple so they can be read aloud by another.

Father, I praise and worship you because you are...

I thank you that...

I confess that I...

and I ask that...

Father, I also ask that you...

Amen.

We tell people they do not have to complete every line, but we usually find they are keen to use the whole lot. It is important to have people swap prayers, so that they do not feel overwhelmed by the initial experience of saying a longer prayer aloud.

In week six we use the same format, but individuals read their own prayers. By this stage, the pattern of prayer is usually established and people are at ease praying aloud. From week seven onwards we encourage individuals to pray aloud using the basic format, or some element of it, without writing their prayers down. Some people still prefer to write and we allow time for this, so they do not feel they have to pray without preparation.

Encouraging people to pray

Praying in a group is different to praying personally. These differences can be positive and negative, depending on how they are used. The following are some ideas to promote prayer in your group.

✦ Provide leadership in prayer, being an example both during the group and at home. This means consistently allowing time to pray during your group meetings, and praying for others in your group during the week. This communicates that you think it is important enough to actually spend some time doing it.

✦ Make sure prayer actually happens. Your role as a leader is to capitalise on the benefits of praying with others. Since praying corporately requires that people talk before they pray, one of the difficulties is that people can have a tendency to talk more to each other than to God. Make sure people actually talk to God, not just with each other.

✦ Encourage written prayers occasionally. This promotes the practice of praying carefully and deliberately. If you feel that your group members are praying simply to hear the sound of their own voices, this is one intervention you might use.

✦ Give prayer the time it needs, being creative and flexible in timing. Almost every group we have seen in action has prayed at the end of their time. While it is useful to develop a pattern which people are comfortable with, you can also move the prayer time around to give it a greater focus. We have sometimes prayed for personal issues at the beginning of our meeting, linking it to the chatting that happens as people arrive. We have then prayed in response to the study at the end of our time. We know a group where one person is responsible for prayer for that week and he or she simply declares – 'We will pray now'. Whenever that person feels there is a significant point to pray for, he or she declares prayer time. This is useful and creative.

✦ Separate different types of prayer. Sometimes it is a good change to focus on different types of prayer on different nights. Our experience is that most people focus on asking God for their own needs (supplication) and so it is useful to think in different categories. Remember ACTS: Adoration, Confession, Thanksgiving, Supplication. The group can progressively work through each of these categories, or even focus on only one of them for the whole prayer time.

✦ Give special focus to prayer in some sessions. At the end of a series on a book we will occasionally have a prayer night rather than a study. This can be an effective way to summarise or review what has been learned from a series, helping people apply what they have talked about to their spiritual lives. Alternatively, it can be used more generally as a time for a range of prayer. We prepare an outline which provides a structure to the prayer time. It is rare for a totally unplanned session to be beneficial for people.

The program below was prepared for a group that had previously studied Colossians. It took about 20 minutes to devise and has short periods (10 minutes maximum) of prayer in different-sized groups. It introduces a wide range of Bible passages and incorporates things the group has already learned. The structure provides variety while not pressuring people into praying.

Welcome. Describe our night.

Reading: Psalm 19.

Pray in whole group, focusing on God's character.

Reading: Colossians 1:15–20.

Pray in whole group, focusing on Jesus.

Reading: Colossians 1:21–23.

Pray in pairs, thanking God for bringing us to him.

Reading: Colossians 3:1–17.

Pray silently, confessing our sins to God.

Reading: Romans 10:14–15.

Pray in whole group, focusing on world mission, in particular those associated with our group.

If we had missionary prayer letters we would also use them. If possible, over coffee we would write postcards to those we prayed for. Other prayers might include focusing on our local community, our church, local ministries and many other things.

✦ Follow through on people's prayers. It can be helpful to keep a prayer book in which to record, in point form, the group's prayers. It is one person's responsibility each week to follow up on prayers from the previous weeks. Ticking previous prayers or recording answers to prayers is also encouraging. Explaining the reasons behind such activities also encourages people to do the same in their own times of prayer. Checking the prayer book can be incorporated into a meeting devoted to prayer, either as the source of thanksgiving for those answered or for ongoing supplication if necessary.

✦   Form prayer partners or triplets. In larger groups we have formed prayer partners or triplets who pray together during each meeting. Before we break up to pray we ask if there are general points which we all need to pray for, and then people share their personal requests in their triplets.

We do not suggest you do this during the forming stage of the group's life, since corporate prayer actually builds the group and establishes relationships and trust. However, once the group has been established you can split into smaller groups.

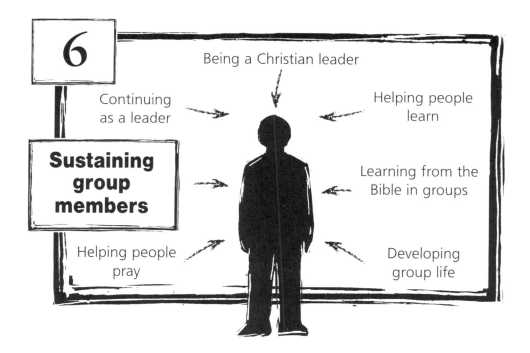

6

Sustaining group members

Being a Christian leader

Continuing as a leader

Helping people learn

Learning from the Bible in groups

Helping people pray

Developing group life

The underlying assumption in all we have written so far is that you are aiming to help group members grow in their relationship with God. Being a Bible study group leader involves looking after people and caring for them pastorally. This chapter fits at this point within the overall model because our care for people will be shaped by our understanding of Christian leadership; our commitment to helping people learn from Scripture; and the contribution of mutual support within a well-functioning and prayerful group.

The goal of pastoral care

Our commitment to people grows out of our understanding of Christian leadership. As we stated in the first chapter, we are looking after God's people because he gave them to us as part of his flock. Since each of these people is loved by God and is important to him, he or she must also be important to us. We care for people because God cares for them. We care for them as an expression of our love for them. Earlier, we referred to the sixteenth century theologian Martin Bucer, who said a pastor's purpose was:

1. to draw to Christ those who are alienated.

2. to lead back those who have been drawn away.

3. to secure amendment of life for those who fall into sin.

4. to strengthen weak and silly Christians.

5. to preserve Christians who are whole and strong and urge them forward to the good.[1]

This description is equally applicable to Bible study group leaders. We are pastoring a portion of God's flock, and in doing so we are attempting all the things described above. Our aim is to take people from wherever they are and move them towards Christ. The goal is to produce mature, whole, integrated Christians; all the time recognising that it is God who brings about change. This combination of God's work and our efforts means, while we are accountable to God, we are not held responsible by him for other people's growth. In the end, we are each responsible before God for our own spiritual growth.

The nature of Bible study groups is that we are dealing with all types of people in their relationships with Christ. We can never assume all our group members are at the same place in their spiritual walk, and so we must be aware of their different requirements. We have found there are five basic types of people who participate in our groups. They are

1. not yet Christians;

2. young or weak Christians;

3. growing in faith;

4. spiritually dry;

5. mature serving believers.

The 'not yet Christians' are those investigating Jesus or who consider themselves to be Christian but are not actually converted. The 'young or weak Christians' are those who have a personal faith but are not very far in their journey as believers, or who are not actually progressing at all. Those 'growing in faith' are the keen Christians who are embracing their Lord and striving to grow, and the 'spiritually dry' are those who have a mature faith but are

---

1.　M. Bucer, *Martini Bucer Opera Omnia Series 1: Deutsche Schriften,* Vol 7, 67-245 in D. Tidball, *Skilful shepherds* (Leicester: IVP, 1986), 47.

currently experiencing a loss of vitality and intimacy with God. 'Mature serving believers' are those who have grasped the significance of helping others grow in their relationship with Christ.

Deciding where people are at

What do you look for when considering members of your group and the best way to minister to them?

The aim of Bible study groups is to help all participants become mature serving believers, taking them from where they are and moving them forward. To do this, you need to know where they are currently. We don't expect that you will sit your group down and interrogate each of them – rather that you would be conscious of where people are at as you speak to individuals and listen to their comments, so you can determine how best to serve them. Having made an assessment, we recommend you never publicise it, and be prepared to reconsider as people change.

A friend told us the story of an older clergyman who said Jesus warned against judging others, while also saying 'by their fruit you will know them'. In his wisdom, the clergyman said 'Jesus didn't call us to be judges, but he did call us to be fruit inspectors'.

But you may well ask: 'How do you determine which people fall into which group?' This is an important question, and you will hear clues as you listen to people in the group. The place to begin is to identify any non-Christians in your group. Often they will have been open about this before joining the group, or you could ask some tactful questions while chatting over supper. Also try to identify Christians who do not seem to understand the basics of faith. Respect their claim to be Christian, but do not be afraid to question them further. 'What impact has being a Christian had on your life?' If the question draws a confused answer, or it indicates a lack of understanding with comments such as 'I am not a very good Christian', then you can move backwards to 'If you died tonight, what would you say to God when he asked why you should be allowed into heaven?'

If on the other hand you draw a positive response to your first question, you might ask probing questions about prayer, Bible reading, church and ministry to determine whether the person falls into group 2 or 3. Remember not to be deceived by the length of time someone has been a Christian. There are many immature Christians who were converted a long time ago, and there are many recent converts who are already well along their spiritual journey and in the 'growing in faith' category.

The last questions you would ask clarify a person's current spiritual journey and relationship with Christ, and whether he or she is actually progressing. These issues would encompass the person's experience of joy, hope, forgiveness and love, and identify whether he or she is in group 4 or 5.

> What are you involved in?
>
> What do you want to be involved in?
>
> What do you support financially?
>
> What do you regularly pray for?

These questions would revolve around people's experience of faith and their commitment to their church or para-church organisation, their use of money and spare time. Explore people's reasons for the things they do. This identifies those who are seeking self-aggrandisement or who are driven by guilt, and those who genuinely want to serve and glorify Christ in all aspects of their lives.

We are not suggesting you quiz people in the first meeting, and if you have done some exercises which elicit this information then you may not need to explore further. The exercises you could use would be 'testimonies' and 'lifelines'. These are explained in Chapter 4: 'Developing group life'. If you have not done exercises of this type then you may like to keep in mind the general questions mentioned above.

There are many factors involved in understanding where people are at spiritually. However, a good place to start is to examine their knowledge of the truth and its application to their lives. This reflects Paul's prayer in Colossians 1:9–10 that the Colossians may be filled with the knowledge of God's will in all spiritual understanding and wisdom, so that they might lead lives worthy of the Lord. These factors can be compared on the following grid:

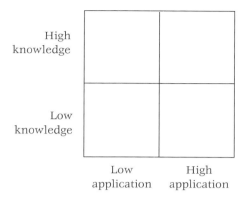

We call this grid the Maturity Matrix. It identifies the possible combinations of knowledge and application. There are four possible positions on the grid:

high knowledge, high application;

high knowledge, low application;

low knowledge, high application;

low knowledge, low application.

None of these positions is intrinsically 'bad', but we want to help people move to the high knowledge – high application position. Then they will have a thorough understanding of the Bible and it will be having a significant effect on their lives.

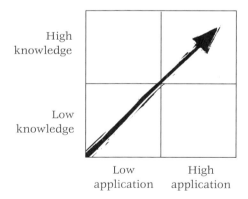

While it is simplistic to equate a high knowledge of the Bible with a high knowledge of truth, we believe knowledge of the Bible is a prerequisite for knowledge of the truth. We are aiming for a position where people have read the Bible carefully and are seeking to apply it to every sector of their lives. This is the desire of Paul's prayer for the Colossians.

In the **high knowledge – low application** position, people have a deep knowledge of the Bible, but they don't apply it to their lives. This is dangerous knowledge which can easily puff up and lead to arrogance. They do not understand that their lives should change as a result of their knowledge. This can lead to problems for a Bible study group, as an extensive knowledge of the Scriptures can masquerade as, or be misinterpreted as, Christian maturity. As leaders we need to be aware of this issue, and ensure that these people are challenged to live out what they know.

In the **low knowledge – high application** square are people who do not have much knowledge of the Bible, but all they know they are applying in their lives. Some simply need to be encouraged to keep on learning. This is not difficult, since they have a natural desire to learn. Our role as leaders is to feed and nurture them on the Word. These people are a delight to have in a group as they respond to an increasing knowledge of Scripture like a flower opening in the sun. However, there are also some in this category who regard it as virtuous to have a limited knowledge of Scripture. They say they do not want to have an academic faith, but simply want to love and serve the Lord. While this may sound pious, it isn't. It assumes that God can be known without listening to him speak. It assumes that once you enter into a relationship with God you do not need to learn more about who he is and how we relate to him as his people. As leaders we need to warn these people about serving a God created in their own image, and challenge them to worship and serve God as he makes himself known in the Bible.

In the **low knowledge – low application** position are people who have recently become Christians, or who have become stuck in their spiritual journeys. In 1 Corinthians 3, Paul talks about Christians who should have been eating meat but were only able to handle milk. Your group program should reflect the maturity of the members of the group. Do not choke people with meat they cannot handle, and do not undernourish those who should be eating more substantial things. It may be better to form separate groups when the needs of members are too diverse, rather than trying to feed all people with one meal.

We have led groups for young Christians and have found them a great joy. Leaders need to feed young Christians on Scripture and encourage and nurture them as they respond to what they learn. We recommend you only have a separate group for a maximum of twelve months, and strive to incorporate the young Christians into regular groups as quickly as possible.

Dealing with those who are stuck is hard, but an effective group can often really help people. Sometimes people have not grown because they have not been fed, and sometimes they have not had any examples or role models to follow. Simply being in a group can address both these needs. The example and encouragement of others who are keen and progressing is a great challenge and stimulus, even to those who are not stuck. When someone has been a Christian for a long time and does not seem to have progressed in faith, it is important to work out what is preventing his or her progress and address whatever it is. Often people lack a full appreciation of God's grace, so we suggest you explore this as a starting point. Remember also that God sometimes uses experiences of staleness to call us away from our past securities, success and complacency.

Basic skills for looking after people

Think back over your experience as a growing Christian. What things did you need, to help you keep growing? What did you receive that helped you to grow?

1. Perseverance and hard work

Consider your own spiritual growth. We assume it has not happened without hard work. If you are helping others in their growth, it will also take perseverance and hard work. Many times we have given up on helping people grow, or wanted to give up on them, only to see them a few years down the track growing and persevering for themselves. We have been encouraged to discover that God has a longer time frame than we have. He perseveres with people and helps them to grow long after we have given up. God will bring to completion the work he has begun in us.

This does not mean that
we think a person's life
is one long upward
movement towards
maturity and an
excellent relationship
with God.

We think it is something quite different. Bill Hybels explained it simply at a conference when he said, 'Rather than our spiritual life looking like a continual upward journey, it is more accurate to think of it as a series of stages'.

In our spiritual lives we go up for a while, learning, growing and changing.

Then we plateau during a period of coasting and assimilating the things we have learned.

After this we have a period of crisis or doubt.

This prompts us into further growth.

Over time, it would look like this:

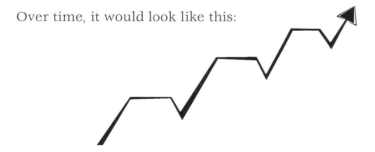

This model helps us to persevere with ourselves and to weather the crises in other people's lives. It also encourages us that the latest crisis is not the end of our faith, but rather an intrinsic part of its growth.

2. A model for understanding people

A framework for considering human behaviour provides a foundation for analysing what is happening in a group. An awareness and recognition of how different personalities work can help you determine the most appropriate way of handling issues. We have found the Myers-Briggs Type Indicator (MBTI)[2] and the work of Larry Crabb and Dan Allender[3] very helpful in understanding people.

The MBTI looks at the individual preferences which shape personalities. We all have preferences: whether we write with our left or right hand, whether we cross our arms left over right or right over left, whether we choose mango or chocolate. These preferences shape how we operate. The MBTI is based on the work of Swiss psychologist, Carl Jung, who argued that people have preferences in the way they think. He argued that thinking involves gathering information and making decisions. He claimed that our preferences in how we approach these two tasks shape our personality:

> Some people prefer gathering information from their five senses, while others prefer to use intuition.

> Some people prefer making decisions based on logic, while others prefer to be guided by their values and beliefs.

> People tend to be internally or externally focused.

Jung argued that our preferences profoundly influence the way we operate as individuals. The MBTI identifies a range of personality styles by considering people's inclination for different preferences.

---

2.   *Introduction to type,* 5th edition (Palo Alto: Consulting Psychologist Press, 1993) by Isabel Briggs Myers is a concise introduction to the MBTI.

3.   L. J. Crabb Jr. and D. B. Allender, *Encouragement: The key to caring* (Grand Rapids: Zondervan, 1984).

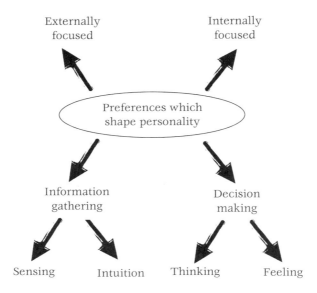

The benefit of this model is that it explains why people will sometimes do things which we find very frustrating. People who prefer being **externally focused** love groups and are greatly energised by being in them, while those who are **internally focused** often find groups tiring and draining. Externally focused people often learn best through interaction and discussion, tending to speak first and reflect later, while internally focused people tend to reflect first and speak later, preferring to think deeply and enjoying the opportunity to dwell on their thoughts.

People who prefer **sensing** as the basis for information gathering like to know specific facts and details, while those who prefer **intuition** like developing a big picture and exploring the connections between ideas. For the intuitive person, getting bogged down in details is a great frustration, while lack of detail is equally frustrating for the sensate.

Those who prefer **thinking** as the basis of making decisions like detached objectivity and analytical logic, while those preferring **feelings** value person-centred decisions which understand and appreciate personal values and beliefs.

Finally, people who prefer **information gathering** over decision making will often want to gather more detail before making a decision, preferring to keep an open mind, while those preferring **decision making** like reaching conclusions and having closure. In groups, this means some will want to keep talking and discussing, while others decided twenty minutes earlier what they thought and are now waiting to move on.

How people participate in a group is a function of their personalities. The MBTI helps us consider whether what we perceive to be a problem in a group may actually be a result of personality differences which need to be accommodated rather than corrected. It is beyond the scope of this book to explore this area in detail, but personality differences also affect how we express our spirituality. As leaders, we need to ensure that we do not decide someone is immature simply because they are different.

The weakness of the MBTI is that it does not take account of human sinfulness. Therefore, it is important also to have a model which helps us understand how we operate as sinful people, to add to what we have already learned about personality types. This is where the work of Crabb and Allender is helpful. They identify fear of rejection as the core emotion of people, with self protection as the primary concern. This leads people to develop protective layers which shield them from rejection. They try to avoid rejection 'by putting their best foot forward ... by wearing protective layers designed to win approval'.[4]

People develop protective layers to shield them from rejection[5]

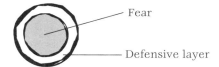

Fear

Defensive layer

Some examples of this are the friendly joker who manages to avoid intimacy by being funny; the helpful person who is never vulnerable and needing the help of others; the person who will never try anything new for fear of failing at it; and the person who plays the role of expert in order to cover his or her insecurity. Such behaviour can lead to Christian fellowship consisting only of superficial interaction between our protective layers. People play the roles they think others expect or which they hope will win acceptance and approval.

---

4.   Crabb & Allender, 36.
5.   Crabb & Allender, 34.

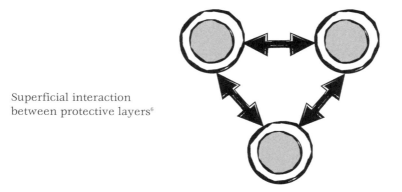

Superficial interaction
between protective layers[6]

The implications of this for pastoral ministry are fully explored in *Encouragement* and Crabb's other books, and we recommend you read these as you consider this aspect of Bible study group leading.

Addressing the surface layers will not produce growth. Explaining to the friendly joker that his or her behaviour restricts intimacy does not acknowledge the person's inner fear of rejection which produced the response. Challenging the expert on his or her desire always to be seen to be right ignores the insecurity associated with being wrong. Conformity, complacency and callousness result as the truth simply bounces off the defensive layers.

Truth without
love bounces off
the protective
layer[7]

Imagine someone afraid that God does not like him or her. The defensive layer could manifest as a complacency about spiritual discipline, or a callousness towards Christianity, or religious conformity. Attacking the protective layers only strengthens the person's desire to hide the real problem. True growth would only occur through discovery that God considers this person to be a treasured possession.

---

6.   Crabb & Allender, 35.
7.   Crabb & Allender, 92.

The main principle is to address the core issues of people's fear rather than their defensive layers, if we really want to help them grow. In particular, their fear needs to be addressed by truth and genuine love.

Love breaks through the protective barrier to address the inner fear[8]

Crabb and Allender remind us that genuine growth happens as we address people's fears and help them appreciate all that Christ accomplished on the cross for them.

Understanding how people construct defensive layers, and learning to identify these, helps us as we care for people. We need to work hard to address the real concerns and fears of people, not just deal with the surface layers.

People need to be provided with security and significance. Both of these are essential for an individual's wellbeing, and ultimately, these can only be found through relationship with Christ. As leaders we need to attempt to provide some measure of security and significance for the members of our group, to enable them to address their inner fears.

3. Communication skills

Communication skills are fundamental in identifying and addressing people's real concerns. Communication is the process by which you express your own views and understand the views of others. Many books have been written on the theory and practice of communication, so we will deal with it here only as it applies to Bible study groups.

An effective leader is keen to promote good communication within the group. Like any other process, communication can be done well or it can be done poorly. Your level of skill as a leader will affect the way in which your group works. People need to feel that the discussion is relevant to where they are at, and they need to feel understood when they make a contribution. If you are unable to clearly express your opinions or help others clarify their thoughts, it is quite likely that people will become frustrated and some may

---

8.   Crabb & Allender, 73.

withdraw from the group. On the other hand, by asking people to use different words to express their views, and to give examples of what they are talking about, you can help them articulate themselves more clearly. Ask others to give summaries, and give feedback about what you understand people have said. This will help create satisfying and rewarding discussions.

The basic model of communication is where one person seeks to convey a message to another. The receiver then tries to return the message (feedback). This sounds simple, but there are many factors which complicate the process. In the diagram below you can see some of the factors which detract from the communication process.

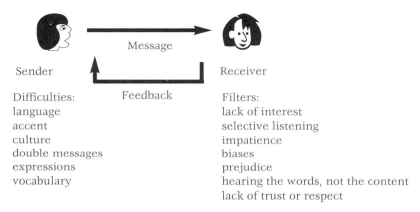

These difficulties and filters need to be taken into account in any interaction. Therefore you need to develop a process where you can check what has been said to ensure that it has been understood.

In any conversation there are six possible messages:

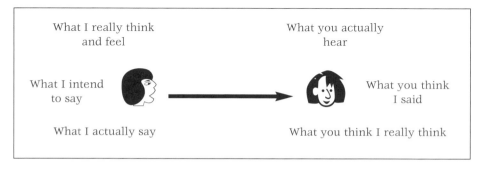

Imagine the two of us talking about how a Bible study went. Karen has enjoyed the study, but she feels frustrated that the discussion went on too long and annoyed because we ran out of time for prayer.

She thinks: 'I'm sick of running overtime talking and then skipping on other things equally important' (what she really thinks); but to be polite she plans to say 'I was disappointed that we ran overtime tonight' (what she wants to put into words). But what she says is 'You need to be more disciplined in leading the discussion' (what she actually puts into words). Rod hears Karen say 'You need to be more disciplined in leading' (what he hears her say). He thinks she is complaining about him not being a good leader (what he thinks she said). Therefore he thinks she thinks he is inadequate as a discussion leader, and that she is embarrassed by him in front of the group (what he thinks she really wanted to say). He feels hurt and Karen is bewildered by his strange reaction.

Notice how the first and last positions are significantly different. The important point here is that this is only the opening statement in the conversation. As it continues, the possibility for misunderstanding increases dramatically. If there have been five exchanges of comments then there are at least thirty possible understandings of what is going on. Therefore it is important that each comment is understood to mean what was intended. People need to work hard at promoting understanding between individuals and among groups. In a group, the channels of communication become even more entangled, so it is even more important to work at ensuring understanding.

Listening

One way to ensure understanding is active listening (also called reflective listening). Active listening involves participating in a conversation: eye contact, nodding, leaning forward. Each of these indicates that you are interested in what the other is saying. Active listening aims to ensure basic understanding of a comment before making a response. It shows you value the statements of other people by checking with them that what you understood is what they intended. Active listening reassures the person talking that you have actually understood what he or she said.

Communicate your grasp of what has been said, by 'reflecting' their statements back to them. You might say:

So you think...

You feel...

Are you saying...

Let me see if I understand...

For instance, Peter says: 'I really hate the way we do this'. You might respond by saying 'So you dislike our practice of asking questions about people's prayer points in this group'. He is then free to respond by saying yes or no, depending on whether you understood accurately. If that is not what he means, there is an opportunity to try again. Peter can reword his statement: 'No, what I meant was that I hate the way we always pray at the end when it's late'. Notice that you do not respond with a further question or a defence, but with a statement which seeks to accurately capture the meaning of the initial comment.

The filters affecting our communication are often invisible to others. If we communicate our comprehension of what was said, it allows the speaker to check that it matches what he or she meant.

The object is to afford other people respect by actually listening to what they say before responding with your own statement or question. Having understood their basic idea you can then probe more deeply by asking further questions. This gives you the freedom to challenge or support, since you understand the person accurately.

Another element of active listening is reporting the emotions you see the other person exhibiting. This could be something like 'The muscles in your face look tense and you seem a bit frustrated'. We have found the phrases 'You seem...' or 'You appear...' to be the best way of reflecting emotions. These give the other person the freedom to say 'No, I've got a toothache and my face is sore', or 'Yes, I'm a bit frustrated because...'. Notice that your attitude is tentative, explaining what you see as well as what you surmise.

Obviously, this technique is ridiculous when overused and applied indiscriminately to every sentence. The aim is to ensure you have captured the main point of what has been said, and to communicate your understanding of it to the other person.

Note that active listening is not simply parroting back to the other person his or her exact words. It is also not a tool to be used to patronise or manipulate another. The principles involved with active listening are:

✦ listening before responding;

✦ letting the other person know you are listening;

✦ letting the other person know what you have understood;

✦ reporting verbal and non-verbal observations.

Observe yourself relating to others and notice the times when you misunderstand their meaning or respond without checking that you have really understood. As you notice these try to reflect back what you have understood and allow the other person to explain again what he or she intended.

Questioning

The skill of asking appropriate questions is critical to looking after your group members. The basic rule of thumb is that people answer the question they are asked. If you ask a closed question, you will get a closed answer. If you ask a question soliciting an opinion then the person will respond with something he or she has thought. If you ask a simple comprehension question then the person will respond in kind.

The most significant idea in learning to ask good questions is the concept of open and closed questions (which we discussed when looking at Bible study questions). You will have experienced these during your life, even though you may not have understood what was happening. Closed questions ask for a specific piece of information, and prompt yes/no responses. Some of the key words forming closed questions are: do, is, are, will, shall. For instance:

> Do you have time?

> Is that your notebook?

> Are you going to the shops?

> Will you pick up that book from the library?

> Shall we go to the movies?

Notice that each of these questions requires only a single word in response. Used excessively, they make a conversation stilted or even abort it completely. Imagine if you were leading a discussion based on these questions:

> Will you count all the times Jesus speaks?

> Is that passage related to this one?

> Do you love people well?

> Are you going to change in response to the passage?

> Shall we have coffee now?

By the time coffee is suggested you would be ready to pack up and go home, as the discussion would be very hard to maintain.

It is easy to fall into the habit of asking closed questions. As a leader, you need to be conscious of any tendency towards this and work hard at using open questions. At times it is appropriate to ask a closed question to clarify an issue, but you need open questions if you wish to promote discussion. Open questions ask the other person to offer an opinion, or make a statement rather than a single word answer. Open questions begin with words like: what, where, when, how, why. For instance:

> What do you want to do tonight?

> Where was the shop?

> When was your holiday?

> How did you react to that?

> Why do you think they did that?

Imagine a discussion based on these questions:

> What was Jesus communicating to his hearers?

> Where did this incident happen?

> When do you think this was recorded?

> How does this affect you and your thinking?

> Why did it affect you that way?

These questions will generate much more discussion than closed questions, and will help people start thinking about the topic at hand. This is also true in our conversation with individuals: the use of closed questions will kill it off quickly, while open questions will promote discussion. Rod recently had a conversation where every question he was asked was a closed question: 'Have you been here before?', 'Did you like the sermon?', 'Do you know many people here?' He was able to stretch these into some sort of conversation, but they were all questions which could have been answered with a simple 'Yes' or 'No'. He asked a series of open questions and received all sorts of information from the other person, but it was a very one-sided conversation, and after twenty minutes he was exhausted and ready to give up.

In summary, the difference between open and closed questions can be seen clearly in the likely responses to these two questions:

> What do you think of God? (open)

> Do you believe in God? (closed)

'What do you think of God?' will secure an opinion and generate interaction. 'Do you believe in God?' will be answered yes or no, and require further questioning to start a discussion.

4. Barbecue skills

The principles involved in having a good conversation at a barbecue also apply to group Bible study and pastoral conversations. We occasionally meet leaders who have difficulty with pastoral care, simply because they have not learned the basic skills of social interaction.

✦ Be polite.

✦ Avoid questions with an obvious or simple answer.

✦ Seek to stimulate discussion. It is all right not to know the answer to a question you ask.

✦ Ask about feelings as well as facts.

✦ Use guiding questions in order to get people to explain further, illustrate, gather opinions from the group.

✦ Periodically summarise the discussion in order to help people keep up the pace and to limit the verbose.

✦ Ask clear, unambiguous questions, that do not need interpretation.

✦ Make questions relevant by dealing with people's true interests rather than abstract ideas.

✦ Ask direct questions of people, especially those who are having trouble breaking into the discussion, but do not humiliate or embarrass them.

✦ Keep responsibility for the discussion within the group. Make them the experts rather than yourself.

✦ Do not judge. Allow people to have a say without fear of ridicule or embarrassment.

✦ Do not preach in a small group. Save it for the pulpit where it rightly belongs.

✦ Set a tone for the group and lead by example. Show interest, be involved, take risks.

✦ Plan ahead. Think about the possible directions that a conversation may take and be aware of potential tangents.

✦ Maintain self-esteem within a group. Watch for any form of denigration, mocking or judgment. Help the group avoid patronising, condescending or sexist comments.

Dealing with conflict

 Recall a conflict you have experienced. Describe each person's point of view. How successful was the resolution? What strategies were used, or could have been used, to resolve it?

Conflict is an integral part of relating and therefore impacts upon small groups. If there were no conflict we would wonder about the depth of relationships in the group. As in marriage, some degree of conflict indicates a healthy level of self-disclosure and truthfulness. We have occasionally heard couples say they have never had a conflict. Instead of encouraging us, it sent us into high anxiety about their relationship. It is the same in groups. If conflict is expected then it is less stressful to deal with. When conflict is treated as the worst thing in the world, it becomes a much bigger problem to overcome. As group leaders, we need to learn how to be in conflict and yet not sin, and to help others in their personal growth with this issue.

Most people readily accept the 'caring' aspects of ministry, but some people have difficulty with confrontation. They feel it is inappropriate to tell people they are wrong or need to change. Our view is that confronting people is an expression of our commitment to helping them become more like Christ.

Jesus was regularly in conflict with others. He cast out the money changers from the temple and he called the Pharisees a brood of vipers (Mark 11:15–17; Matthew 12:34, 23:33). Paul acknowledged that conflict was normal and could be dealt with in either sinful or helpful ways when he said 'Be angry but do not sin; do not let the sun go down on your anger' (Ephesians 4:26). He told the Galatians he was astonished at how quickly they had deserted the true faith (Galatians 1:6). It seems that conflict is a normal part of dealing with sinful people who are not yet completely like Christ, which includes all of us.

In his book *Caring enough to confront*, David Augsburger says 'conflict is natural, normal, neutral, and sometimes even delightful'.[9] He introduces the idea of care-fronting. He works with the dual concepts of loving a person and being willing to confront. He says godly conflict must be both caring and confronting. The following statements illustrate these two aspects:[10]

Caring	Confronting
I care about our relationship.	I feel deeply about the issue at stake.
I want to hear your view.	I want to clearly express mine.
I want to respect your insight.	I want respect for mine.
I trust you to be able to handle my honest feelings.	I want you to trust me with yours.
I promise to stay with the discussion until we have reached an understanding.	I want you to keep working with me until we have reached a new understanding.
I will not trick, pressure, manipulate or distort the differences.	I want your unpressured, clear, honest view of our differences.
I give you my loving, honest respect.	I want your caring confronting respect.

We want to see both caring and confronting within the life of our groups. If we avoid confronting we indicate that we do not really care, while confronting without caring is simply being judge, jury and executioner. The group leader's role is both to care and to confront.

Determine the most appropriate strategy

Some people think there are only two options with conflict: to fight or give in. However there is a range of strategies available to us depending on the relative importance of the issue and the relationship. Sometimes we create problems for ourselves as we approach a conflict without first determining what is important.

---

9. David Augsburger, *Caring enough to confront* (Ventura: Regal Books, 1981), 11.
10. Augsburger, 15.

How important is it that you get what you want? How important is it that the other person gets what he or she wants?[11] Our task as leaders is to determine the most appropriate approach to each particular issue. If an issue is really important to us and we must achieve a particular outcome, we will choose a different strategy than we would if the relationship were really important and we did not particularly care about the outcome. We should **compete** when the outcome is important and the relationship is not. We should **accommodate** when the relationship is important and the outcome is not. We should **avoid** when neither the outcome nor the relationship is important, and **collaborate** when both are.

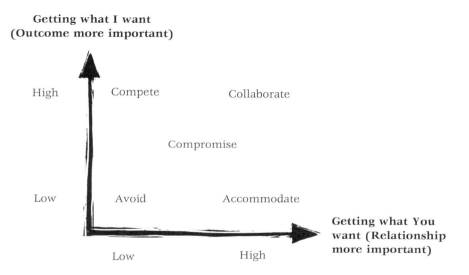

Collaboration is generally the best approach for conflict resolution in a Bible study group. We cannot readily think of a situation in which we would advocate avoidance as a long term strategy. Collaboration acknowledges that both the outcome and the relationship are important, and it encourages mutual problem solving. There are times when the outcome is critical (for instance, understanding the basics of salvation) and these afford no compromise, but even here the importance of fellowship leads us to collaboration as we strive together to understand and obey Scripture. Competition is the last resort which we use only when collaboration has failed and the issue at stake is a gospel truth. Issues like what type of supper we have

---

11. This model is referred to in literature on groups as the Thomas-Kilmann model.

are obviously minor, and we readily accommodate those for whom it is important.

'I' Language

'I' language helps us collaborate and confront cleanly. It is a simple idea which helps us to offer respect and care for another person, while still being able to present our own point of view. It is based upon the fact that when discussions become heated, people tend to attribute to others all sorts of ideas and feelings, and talk as if they know everything the others think and feel. In contrast, using 'I' language involves deliberately trying to describe our thoughts, feelings, and actions, rather than making assumptions about the thoughts, feelings and actions of others. It is a crucial skill if we are going to confront people effectively.

Conflict often expresses itself in 'You' language which attributes thoughts, feelings and intentions to the other person. For instance if Rod was late to meet Karen (a particularly sensitive point for Karen) then she could easily respond like this: 'You idiot, why are you always late to pick me up? You make me feel stupid standing here while everyone else gets picked up!' Notice the number of times the word 'you' is used in this short interchange. It is a reasonably aggressive stance, and can only inflame both people as Rod tries to defend himself.

'I' language demands the speaker speak only for him or herself. Another person cannot make someone feel stupid, angry or sad. The individual chooses to feel that way in response to what is said or done. Some people can try to make a person angry, sad or hurt, but the other person still chooses his or her own response. Therefore if Karen was going to use 'I' language, she could say: 'When you are late I feel angry and stupid standing here for hours. I would prefer you picked me up on time or at least rang me.'

This statement communicates the same frustration, but is not as inflammatory as the previous statement. It also expresses Karen's choice to feel angry and stupid. The name-calling just has to be left out. As in the school playground, name-calling may not break bones but it certainly causes real damage.

Notice there are three parts to the 'I' statement:

1. the action;
2. the response;
3. the preferred outcome.[12]

Karen identifies what specific act has caused the conflict, she identifies what response it has generated within her, and she describes what she would have preferred. In doing this, she provides Rod with an avenue for change.

The fundamental principle of 'I' language is that people speak only for themselves. It is invalid for a person to say:

> You think...
>
> You are...
>
> You feel...

We can never really know these things about another person. Therefore in conflict situations we need to use phrases like:

> I think...
>
> I feel...
>
> I want...

These express information of which we can be confident. 'I' language is particularly important in heated situations. It could be useful explaining this skill and then practising it in your small group to ensure that people are only speaking for themselves.

This idea is developed more fully in *Everyone can win*.[13] This enjoyable book on conflict includes many ideas, stories and suggestions, and is well worth adding to your library.

People/problems

In order to resolve conflict, it is important to deal with the problem rather than accusing people of being problems. This demands the leader keeps a watch on the language of those in conflict. Remind people to focus on the issue and not to stray into personal attacks. In general, people can fix actions and behaviours, but 'fixing' personalities is a much more time consuming and threatening process. Describe a behaviour, action, or attitude, such as: 'You are

---

12. H. Cornelius and S. Faire, *Everyone can win* (Roseville, Australia: Simon and Schuster, 1989), 61.
13. Cornelius and Faire, 60.

often late'; or 'You don't let me finish my sentences'. This enables a person to consider changing the cause of a problem. A personal comment such as 'You're lazy', 'You're selfish', or 'You're hopeless' only leads to problems as people feel attacked and hurt.

You may be wondering about the connection between this idea and the 'I' language concept. It is OK to use 'you' when describing the objective actions and behaviours of another. The danger is when we attribute intentions, motives and feelings, making assumptions about the inner workings of people's minds. These can only be described subjectively by each individual.

Needs, options, agreement

A useful tool for dealing with conflict is the Needs/options/ agreement table. When people argue, they often have specific options in mind and are fighting hard for their particular point of view. It is difficult to come to an agreement when both people are committed to their own position. For example, examine the discussion we had when planning a night out. If our preferences were recorded on paper they would look like this:

Needs	Options	Agreement
	1. Eat at the Italian restaurant and listen to some jazz. (Rod)	Unable to decide!
	2. Eat at the Thai restaurant and go to a movie with friends. (Karen)	

These two options are incompatible, and a compromise would have left both of us dissatisfied. One of us had to give in, or we needed to generate further options which would satisfy us both.

One way of generating further options and moving forward is to go backwards first. Each of our options was based on particular needs which we wanted to fulfil. Therefore if we uncovered these needs we could perhaps reach a mutually acceptable solution. This additional information is shown in the table on the next page.

Needs	Options	Agreement
Eat somewhere cheap. (Rod) Eat where we like the food. (Rod) Go out rather than home. (Rod) Do something fun. (Rod) Eat something spicy. (Karen) Do something low key. (Karen) Do something with people. (Karen)	1. Eat at the Italian restaurant and listen to some jazz. (Rod) 2. Eat at the Thai restaurant and go to a movie with friends. (Karen)	Choose the option that best meets our needs.

Having explored some of the needs underlying our initial options, we can generate further options based on the needs that are most important to us. (In this example our most important needs are in bold print.)

Needs	Options which meet these needs	Agreement
Eat somewhere cheap. (Rod) **Eat where we like the food. (Rod)** Go out rather than home. (Rod) **Do something fun. (Rod)** **Eat something spicy. (Karen)** Do something low key. (Karen) **Do something with people. (Karen)**	1. Eat at the Italian restaurant and listen to some jazz. (Rod) 2. Eat at the Thai restaurant and go to a movie. (Karen) 3. Eat at the Spanish restaurant and go to a friend's house. 4. Eat at the Turkish pizza place and go window shopping.	Choose the option that best meets our needs.

After all this we were able to decide upon eating at the Spanish restaurant and going to a friend's house for coffee. We were both happy with the solution since it fulfilled most of our needs and neither of us had to give in.

This is a simple example, but the principles can be applied to more significant conflicts. We have also found that we can obtain advice from others about how to meet our needs when we have clearly defined what those needs are.

In summary, the steps are to record the different options from different people, and then work backwards to bring to light the needs of each person involved. To work out the needs requires questions such as 'What are you feeling that makes you want your option?' or 'How does your option fulfil your needs?' Having worked out the needs, move forward to generate further options. Once other options are created, it is often easier to find a mutually acceptable solution.

Dealing with conflict in groups

An important aspect of conflict in groups is that it needs to be resolved in the group. This avoids the uncertainty created by hidden unresolved conflicts and 'no-go' areas. If two people have a conflict which is then resolved outside the meeting without further reference to the group, the rest of the group may continue to be tense and this could severely affect the level of trust. Resolve a conflict in the group if at all possible. An alternative is for the people involved to resolve the conflict outside the group and then report back the current situation to the others. This acknowledges the group's involvement, even if they were only observers.

When dealing with conflict it is also important to try to end the group at approximately the normal time. This may mean adjourning the issue temporarily, but notice that adjourning does not mean avoiding. The reason for adjourning is that people soon learn to avoid conflict if they think it means that they will get trapped in an argument that goes on 'forever'.

Dealing with problems

Looking after people will involve dealing with problems, whether they be sin or doubt, apathy or backsliding, guilt or arrogance. Each of these have various issues associated with them, which are explored in depth in the relevant sections of *Christian counselling* by

Gary Collins.[14] We have found this book useful, as each chapter addresses a different issue, offering a coherent, intelligent and biblical response.

It is easy to forget that there are various ways for responding to a problem. The intervention cube, which we examined in Chapter 4: 'Developing group life', can also be applied to dealing with pastoral problems. You will recall the diagram indicating that interventions could vary in intensity, level and type.[15]

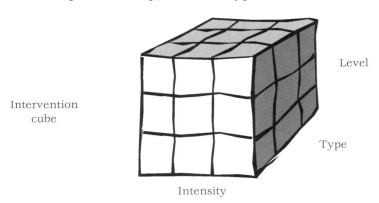

Intervention cube

Level

Type

Intensity

Consider what sort of response will best address a particular problem. Some problems require intensive one-to-one ministry, while others can be addressed by group teaching or the development of an accountability structure. For instance, a young student struggling with lust within male/female relationships may be helped by meeting individually with you, or by participating in a series of group studies, or by ensuring that he or she does not spend time in seductive situations.

Handling another person's sin in a group is an extraordinarily difficult task. We need to keep in mind the principles and procedures outlined in Scripture. Galatians 6 tells us to restore people gently, while taking care not to fall into sin ourselves. 1 Corinthians 5 reminds us of the need to maintain the purity of the church. James 5 emphasises the value of returning people to the truth. Matthew 18 outlines the escalating process of getting others involved in order to bring about repentance.

---

14. Gary Collins, *Christian counselling* (Milton Keynes: Word, 1989).
15. A.Cohen and R. Smith, *The critical incident in group growth* (La Jolla: University Associates, 1976).

Get others involved when necessary

Do not go in over your depth. You will only cause problems for yourself and the person to whom you are ministering. If you consistently feel out of your depth with another person's problems, seek advice early. Find a professional counsellor or minister you trust, and explain what is happening. Take this person's advice if he or she suggests getting other people involved.

It is necessary to get others involved if a group member continues in sin without repentance. This is the process described in Matthew 18, and we believe it requires you to let your minister know when someone in your group is sinning without repentance.

If you realise that an issue surfacing in your group is part of a larger church-wide problem, you also need to talk to your minister, as he or she should be involved in addressing it. A few years ago Rod was concerned about the attitude to alcohol that was developing among a number of students to whom he ministered. He approached each student individually, but he also realised it was a larger issue which was developing as a consequence of misunderstanding grace. The response also required teaching at church level. More recently, we have spoken with people who were not looking forward to heaven. Again, while being an individual issue, it was also a broader issue which required the response of the pastor.

One part of our accountability as leaders is always to do what is best for the whole group. If you have members with serious psychological problems who are severely affecting the functioning of the group, then it is time to seek help. You were not asked to lead in order to be a social worker, counsellor or psychologist, and if that is what people need then you must encourage them to get the professional help they require. You (or someone on your church staff) can help them find appropriate help, but they also need to be responsible for their own psychological wellbeing. There can be very little growth if the only reason they are seeing someone is because they want to please you.

The limit of your responsibility

We have consistently stated that leaders are accountable for helping people grow in their relationship to Christ and in relationship to others. We have also said that people's growth is God's responsibility. You are accountable to God for how you lead, but growth is his work.

Ultimately, the people in the group are God's responsibility, not yours. Therefore there are limits to your accountability. Those limits come into play when the demands upon you are excessive. Since you are also accountable for your own growth in relationship with God, this is a factor in determining where to set the boundary. A good friend once said to Karen, 'If this is making you bitter and ungodly, then, no matter how good it is, it's time to give it up'. We think this is a good general principle. If your group is making you bitter, cynical, ungodly or sinful then it is time to leave or at least get serious help.

Sometimes a person will drop out of a group because of sin in his or her life or some other problem. We find it important to maintain our relationship with such people for as long as possible. This means not rejecting them, but trying to keep relating, even if they stop coming to the group. Asking them to keep telling you what is happening for them indicates a real level of concern and love. Hopefully this will help them return to fellowship. Remember that God has promised to complete what he has begun in people's lives. We must persevere in prayer, trusting God to be faithful to his word. As a leader, you have an ongoing responsibility to pray.

Confidentiality

Confidentiality is important in all groups, but particularly in Bible study groups. If people are to feel free to share their successes, failures and issues, then they must be able to trust that their secrets won't be spread all over the church by next Sunday. This affects the leader more than all the others and so we must be especially careful. Leaders often have contact with many more people in church than a regular member, and therefore have the potential to spread gossip further.

In the first meeting it is good to explore what people want in terms of confidentiality and then make that part of your group's agreement. On the other hand it is important not to promise absolute secrecy before someone has told you what an issue is, as you may need to refer the issue to another or seek advice. If you do offer absolute secrecy then you may find yourself trapped into dealing with an issue beyond your scope.

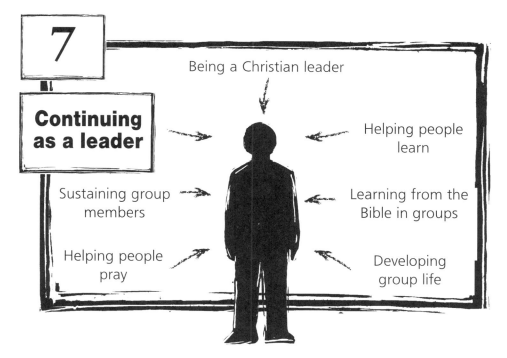

7

Continuing as a leader

Being a Christian leader

Helping people learn

Sustaining group members

Learning from the Bible in groups

Helping people pray

Developing group life

A t a training course for group leaders, Rod asked people how long they had been leading a Bible study group. One woman indicated that she had been leading a group ever since it formed as a follow-up to the 1959 Billy Graham Crusade in Sydney. Nearly forty years of ongoing leadership is a wealth of experience! Rod, who has only been a Christian for twenty years, realised that perhaps this woman should have been conducting the training course and he should have been the student.

Some readers may be in a similar situation to the woman who had led a group for so many years. Others who are only just starting on the road of group leadership might continue to lead for many years and become like her. It is our prayer that you do.

What does an experienced Bible study group leader need in order to continue effectively as a leader?

We are aware of many leaders who have started with great enthusiasm but have grown weary and disillusioned over time. Some people feel as if they have been given a task beyond their ability, with little care, attention or support. Although they have struggled along, they are discouraged and spent. This final chapter moves beyond the issues associated with initial training, and considers those related to continuing and progressing as a leader over time. It explores how to progress as a leader once you have developed reasonable competence in the role.

Refreshment

One of the dangers of Bible study group leadership is that you are often giving of yourself and not necessarily receiving and being fed. A minimum requirement for continuing as a leader is to nurture and sustain your own faith. We have commented on this already. Please do not lead others if your own walk with Christ is feeble and undernourished. You may well be able to maintain a convincing facade, but you won't really help your group and you will probably damage yourself.

Bible study group leaders are often also key members on church committees, active leaders of youth groups and Sunday schools, committed to missionary and other Christian societies, busy with work and family commitments, and generally trying to do all they can to serve Christ in every aspect of their lives. This is a great thing, and we want to encourage people to seek out opportunities for ministry and service. However, you need to build a framework of activity that is sustainable over time.

Some leaders simply need a rest. They need time out to relax with family and friends. They need the opportunity to read for spiritual refreshment and recreation. If this is you, it may be that the best way to progress as a leader is by having a break.

In addition to the responsibility of leadership, some leaders have an extra burden created by the fact that there is no end point to their obligation. They became leaders at some point in the past and they are to continue in the role *ad infinitum*. We suggest you consider spending one year in six as a member of a group without the responsibility of leadership. Having a break is refreshing for you, and it also helps the members of a group to move on and change. While we hope that everything we do as leaders is beneficial for the group, it is possible for groups to stagnate, and for us as leaders to contribute to the maintenance of this status quo. Consequently we encourage groups to change every two years, and recommend that a group never last longer than five.

Supervision

One of the questions we are regularly asked is: 'What do we do to help us keep going as experienced Bible study group leaders?' There are many ideas about training as leaders in order to equip people for a new role, but it is a struggle to know what to do once we are competent, experienced and performing well. In addition, it is often frustrating to be expected to attend training and read books designed to teach what we already know. Often experienced leaders do not attend leader's meetings, and are critical of attempts to train them. The answer to this problem may be supervision. This is a practice used within professional helping roles as a way of supporting people and ensuring their effectiveness.

Supervision involves meeting with someone to talk and pray. It is based on the premise that experienced and competent people do not need to be taught basic skills, but still require nurture and encouragement, and the opportunity to reflect on their practice.

The basic rule in finding the right supervisor is to look for someone who is competent as a Bible study group leader and committed to this form of ministry. He or she must be someone with whom you can communicate easily, someone you trust enough to talk to honestly, and someone you respect enough to listen to and value his or her opinion. You need someone who is willing to commit and be available to meet with you, and you need someone who will maintain the confidentiality of what is discussed.

Our first suggestion would be your minister, but it may be that he or she lacks the necessary skills or credibility. It may even be that your minister lacks the conviction that Bible study groups are a worthwhile endeavour. In this case, find someone else. Our second suggestion would be other leaders in your church, or people who have led in the past but who are not currently leading, or possibly even leaders from groups at another church in your area. A final suggestion would be to approach people employed by an agency which promotes Bible study groups, such as the denominational education department or Scripture Union.

Obviously, going outside the normal structures of a ministry has political implications. We would warn you to be diplomatic and discreet, but we encourage you to do whatever is necessary to help you lead your group in the best possible manner. Ultimately, you are accountable to God and therefore you should seek whatever support you need in order to do a job which is pleasing to him.

You can use supervision to achieve a wide range of goals. We suggest you meet with someone regularly with some of these goals in mind:

✦   to gain support and encouragement;

✦   to receive prayer for yourself and your group members;

✦   to discuss difficulties before they develop into problems;

✦   to provide a mechanism for accountability;

✦   to determine if objectives and goals are being met;

✦   to consider how to improve the overall functioning of the group;

✦   to assess whether the group is correctly focused on studying the Bible;

✦   to improve your practice by interaction and discussion with someone else.

The focus and nature of supervision will vary over time, as the group changes and as you grow in competence and confidence. A supervision session would normally involve 30–60 minutes discussion, followed by a time of prayer for yourself and the group members. We suggest you meet for supervision at least twice a year, although quarterly meetings are probably the most beneficial. Some people find a monthly meeting helpful, but this may create too great a time commitment. Meeting individually may be preferable for you, although some people find a small group of three or four more profitable.

What to consider in supervision

As a leader, you should expect to grow and develop with experience. You should expect to develop a repertoire of skills and abilities and increase in confidence over time. However, this takes patience. It does not happen overnight.

Healthy performance is where you operate at a level consistent with your ability. The following diagram illustrates the relationship between what you can reasonably achieve and your level of experience. As your experience increases, so does your ability.

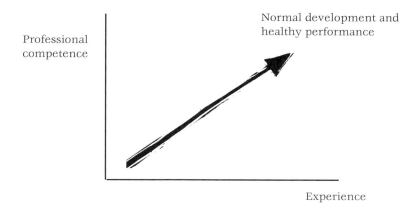

The alternatives to healthy performance are the leaders who try to do more than they are able to, and the ones who do less than they can. The consequences are burnout and boredom, respectively. A leader performing above his or her level of development will need to pretend, and this facade and role playing eventually leads to burnout. The leader performing below his or her level of development tends to get bored over time, and this may lead to complacency, negligence, or even withdrawal from the role. This is represented below. As a leader you need to guard against both.

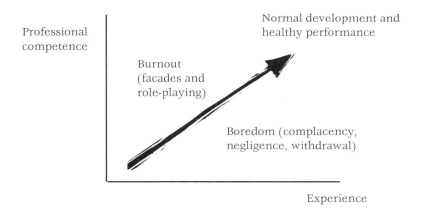

As a leader's needs change, the appropriate style of supervision changes. Early on, you require instructing for your role. Over time this need changes and your supervisor should act more in a coaching relationship. This is followed by a mentoring role. Eventually, as an experienced leader you are a peer to the supervisor, and therefore your relationship becomes one where you consult the supervisor.

Given your changing needs, supervision can focus on a range of areas depending on its goal. There are however four essential areas which always need attention in supervision. These are yourself as a leader, the people in your group, the way the group functions, and the way in which these combine to accomplish the overall goal of the group. For convenience, we remember these as the person, the people, the process, and alignment, which we draw as three sections of a triangle which meet in the centre.[1]

Within the broad framework of person, people, process and alignment, there are multiple issues which require attention. These are listed around the edge of the triangle.

These are not equally significant, but each deserves attention at some point in the supervision process. We recommend you use these as a starting point when meeting with someone for supervision. The triangle has been growing over time as we acknowledge the need to include additional areas, so you should feel free to include items which we have not yet identified.

---

1. This model was developed from one used by the Family Life Movement of Australia for the supervision of its Marriage Educators.

In the ***person*** section we consider the following:

✦ **Character**
Are you growing as a Christian and living a godly and disciplined life?

✦ **Competence**
Do you have the necessary skills and abilities to lead your group?

✦ **Confidence**
Are you confident in your ability to perform your role?

✦ **Commitment**
Are you committed to the group and its members, and is this realistic considering your family, church and work commitments?

✦ **Caring**
Do you demonstrate commitment to caring for the group members?

✦ **Convictions**
Are you convinced about the Bible and its role in the group?

✦ **Prayer**
Do you pray?

In the ***people*** section we are interested in:

✦ **Participation**
Are people regularly attending and participating?

✦ **Discipline**
Are people living out their faith in godly and obedient lives?

✦ **Prayer**
Are people praying?

✦ **Growth**
Are people growing?

✦ **Witness**
Are people witnessing to those around them at work and other places?

✦ **Potential**
Are people being developed for future ministry?

In the ***process*** section we consider:

+ **Content**
  Is the Bible being studied in an appropriate manner?

+ **Structure**
  Is the group structured in a way that facilitates its goals?

+ **Group interaction**
  Is the group session constructively interactive?

+ **Prayer**
  Is the group praying in response to the Bible, in praise, for needs, and for outreach?

+ **Administration**
  Does the administration of the Bible study group ministry adequately support the group?

+ **Training and support**
  Is there a need for special training or support?

As we mentioned earlier, these are not of equal weight. With leaders we supervise, we are always interested in character, content, prayer, discipline, growth and witness, while we occasionally discuss other issues such as administration, training and support, and confidence.

Alignment refers to how all the pieces fit together as a coherent whole. In a sense, it is the 'gut feelings' or intuitive part of supervision. As a supervisor, it means thinking about the total picture and whether everything 'seems' OK. While it is sometimes hard to specify, there are occasionally times where all the pieces appear OK and yet the whole picture doesn't add up. This should act as a warning bell to your supervisor, and encourage him or her to dig deeper and ask more probing questions.

Supervision is a response to the need to encourage and support leaders. It recognises the necessity for ongoing involvement between Bible study leaders and the minister. We believe supervision is best done when it recognises your competency as a leader and responds to you where you are at, while still addressing the range of issues implicit in Bible study group leadership. The following list of questions can be used as a basis for discussion with your supervisor.

SUPERVISION PREPARATION QUESTIONS

Instructions

These questions are for your personal development only. They are not a test or judgment, but will help you identify your strengths and the areas in which your group leadership can be enhanced. Work through and complete each exercise. Write your response so that you can review it at a later time or discuss it with your supervisor.

1. The group

Define the purpose of the group.

Write a description of the group.

Describe the strengths and weaknesses of the group.

Identify what the group has achieved.

Outline any issues that this group will need to address in the future.

2. The process

Write ten words which best describe your group.

Identify the most significant happenings in the life of the group and explain how they were dealt with.

Analyse the ongoing impact that these incidents have had.

Describe the level of trust within the group.

Explain how feedback is provided in the group.

Describe how members of the group communicate with each other.

3. The members

List the main concerns of the participants in the group.

Explain why people became members of this group.

Identify the similarities and differences between people in the group.

Consider the effect of these similarities and differences.

Consider how people are benefiting from the group.

4. The leader

Describe your role in the group.

Explain why you took on the role of leader.

Describe how you feel about the group, and the frustrations and joys you have had in working with the group.

Describe your relationship with the other members of the group, and discuss how it affects your leadership.

Describe how you prefer to learn, and consider how it is reflected in your leadership of the group. Consider how you have tried to accommodate the way others learn.

Identify what you are struggling with at the moment as a group leader.

Describe your preparation for this group.

Evaluate how prayerful you have been for the members of this group.

Consider whether you have been too responsible, or not responsible enough, for what has happened in the group.

State what you think members of the group would say about your leadership.

Explain how you could improve what you do.

5. The context

Discuss any issues related to power, position or control within the group.

Discuss how situations outside the group are affecting it.

6. Future action

Judge the success of this group.

Judge your effectiveness in your role.

Consider if there are any assumptions underpinning your practice which may need to change.

Review your answers to these activities and identify the issues which need further work. Develop a plan for addressing each of these issues.

Peer appraisal process

An alternative to supervision is the peer appraisal process. This process was developed for adult educators who worked independently of each other but needed support and input from others in their field in order to develop professionally. We think the process can be used successfully as a form of peer supervision, if you are committed to working through it fully.

Step 1 involves meeting with a small group of colleagues to reflect on your current practice and identify issues you would like to consider further. Select one of these and agree on the information to collect. For example, you might focus on your questioning skills, collecting information on how many times you answer your own questions, or how regularly you use closed questions when seeking explanations from the group.

Step 2 is to spend an appropriate length of time gathering data on the selected issue.

Step 3 is to meet together with the small group and present your findings to them as critical friends, getting their reactions and feedback.

Step 4 is to reflect on this feedback, and plan the changes you would like to implement as a consequence of the data you gathered and the feedback you received.

Step 5 involves implementing these changes, and observing the impact the changes have on your practice.

Step 6 is to monitor the impact of changes and repeat the cycle from Step 1 as necessary.

Reflection and self appraisal

Having stressed the value of supervision and meeting with others, it is important not to discount reflection and self appraisal as useful tools for developing as a leader. Below are some tools you could use to help you reflect. Allow yourself enough time to complete the activity, and ask yourself the hard questions which you might otherwise ignore. The end of the year particularly is a good time to reflect on small group leadership.

The following activities will help you as you evaluate the year and consider plans for the future. Try to find a quiet hour or so in which you can work through these activities, writing down your thoughts and praying, both for yourself as a group leader and for those who have participated in your group during the year. If possible, share your answers with another group leader with whom you can pray.

Review questions

1. Describe the strengths and weaknesses of your group. What are the things you would like to see repeated next year, and what are the things you hope never to see again?

2. Make a list of your frustrations and joys, the things of which you are proud and the things about which you are sorry.

3. Identify the most significant happenings in the life of the group, and explain how they were dealt with. Consider what ongoing impact these incidents had.

4. Write notes on each of the following issues: clarity of purpose, understanding of interdependence, trust and respect, cohesion, feedback and problem solving.

5. Identify the main achievements of the group.

6. Give your group a score out of ten for each of the following areas:

    ✦   prayerfulness and reverence for God;

    ✦   commitment to studying Scripture;

    ✦   faithful handling of the Bible;

    ✦   discipleship and applying what is learned;

    ✦   evangelistic concern and outreach;

    ✦   missionary concern and support;

    ✦   fellowship;

    ✦   concern for the local community;

    ✦   support for the wider church.

7. List the main concerns of members in the group, and identify how these have been addressed during the year. How has each group member grown during the year?

8. How have you benefited from the group? In what ways have you grown?

9.   Consider how you prefer to learn, and assess how this has been reflected in your leadership of the group. How have you accommodated the learning preferences of others in the way the group is run?

10.   Describe the preparation of yourself and others for group meetings.

11.   Evaluate how prayerful you have been for the members of the group.

12.   Are there any issues related to power, position or control which are affecting the group?

13.   Are there any unresolved issues (for example, conflict between members, or unrepentant sin) which need to be addressed?

14.   State what you think members of the group would say about your leadership.

15.   State what you think God would say about your leadership. Is there anything about it which requires repentance?

SWOT analysis

SWOT analysis is a management technique used to help companies plan and respond to opportunities. It involves considering four areas: strengths, weaknesses, opportunities and threats. SWOT analysis can also be used for reflecting on your group, by considering each of these questions about the group and your leadership:

✦   What are the strengths of this group?

✦   What are the weaknesses of this group?

✦   What are the opportunities for further growth within the group?

✦   What are the threats to the spiritual wellbeing of the members of this group?

✦   What are the strengths of my leadership?

✦   What are the weaknesses of my leadership?

✦   What are the opportunities for further growth in my leadership?

✦   What are the threats to the spiritual wellbeing of myself as leader?

This is only the first step in the process of analysis. Once you have completed these questions, plan ways of overcoming the weaknesses and threats and utilising the strengths and opportunities, either by talking with somebody else, reading further or writing down your own ideas.

Leadership biography

Writing a 'biography' of your development as a group leader is a useful reflection exercise. It requires you to write about yourself in the third person and then read the biography as though it is about someone else, so not everyone will enjoy this or find it profitable. This technique makes use of the anomaly that we can often give advice to others, whereas we struggle to give ourselves the same advice in a similar situation.

Step 1 is to write a short account of how you have developed as a Bible study group leader. Discuss how and why you became a group leader, why you continue in it, and note how you have developed in the role. Write about 'he' or 'she', rather than 'I'. Note the 'highs and lows', the 'challenges and triumphs', the 'joys and disappointments', the 'prouds and sorries', the 'do agains and never agains'.

Step 2 involves reading the biography as if it were the story of another, and identifying the questions you would like to ask the writer, in order to gain a better understanding of what has been described.

Step 3 is to ask those questions of yourself and answer them.

Step 4 is to respond to the biography. Considering the answers given to the questions, what comments would you make to the person who was the subject of the biography, and what advice would you give that person regarding further development?

An alternate process is for Steps 2 and 3 to be done with another – a critical friend. If so, they are not to give their judgment of your biography or of you, rather they are to ask exploratory questions to help you gain a greater understanding of the biography.

Some comments for those responsible for supervision

If you are responsible for other leaders, either as their minister or as a Bible study group coordinator, you should consider supervision as a means for role-modelling pastoral care and also ensuring the alignment of Bible study groups to the overall direction of the ministry. Some people dislike the term supervision, as it carries connotations of authority and control, so you may prefer to use mentoring, consulting or advising. We use supervision, as we like the idea of accountability and deliberate checking.

If you have responsibility for supervising others, here are some suggestions to help:

- ✦ See supervision as an opportunity for quality time with key lay leaders. Form a small group of four or five leaders, and meet with them every three to four months for supervision and prayer over coffee and desert.

- ✦ Make a commitment to doing it. Leaders require supervision at least twice, possibly three times a year, but rarely receive it in the busyness of life. One way to ensure they receive adequate support is to programme meetings at the start of the year. The meetings then become a commitment in your diary, ensuring they happen.

- ✦ We suggest forming groups for supervision based on people's level of experience. Sorting leaders into peer groups and helping people who are each wrestling with similar issues is easier than dealing with large, diverse groups.

- ✦ Use the supervision triangle as a framework to ensure you deal systematically with the needs of your leaders. You may also like to recommend this chapter to your experienced leaders as a starting point in the process.

- ✦ Separate carefully your training and supervision. Everyone needs regular and systematic supervision, but only those who need to learn the basics require training.

Resources for Bible study group leadership

As we have stressed throughout this book, being a Bible study group leader involves bringing together a range of skills and abilities. We recommend you develop a reference library of the following books, which cover the full range of issues associated with Bible study group leadership.

1. Being a Christian leader

Peter Adam, *Speaking God's words* (London: IVP, 1996).

John Stott, *Guard the gospel* (London: IVP, 1973).

Derek Tidball, *Skilful shepherds* (London: IVP, 1986).

2. Helping people learn

Anton Baumohl, *Making adult disciples* (London: SU, 1984).

P. Honey and A. Mumford, *Using your learning styles* (Berkshire: Maidenhead, 1986).

Earl Palmer, Roberta Hestenes and Howard Hendricks, *Mastering teaching* (Portland: Multnomah, 1991).

3. Learning from the Bible in groups

Don Carson, Douglas Moo and Leon Morris, *An introduction to the New Testament* (Leicester: Apollos, 1992).

William J. Dumbrell, *The faith of Israel* (Leicester: Apollos, 1989).

Gordon Fee and Duncan Stuart, *How to read the Bible for all it's worth* (Michigan: Zondervan, 1982).

Graeme Goldsworthy, *According to plan* (Leicester: IVP, 1991).

Graeme Goldsworthy, *Gospel and Kingdom* (Exeter: Paternoster, 1981).

Howard Hendricks and William Hendricks, *Living by the Book* (Chicago: Moody, 1991).

Roberta Hestenes, *Using the Bible in groups* (Philadelphia: Westminster, 1983).

Andrew Reid, *Postcard from Palestine,* 2nd ed. (Sydney: St Matthias Press, 1997).

Mark Strom, *Days are coming* (Sydney: Hodder and Stoughton, 1989).

4. Developing group life

Jarlath Benson, *Working more creatively with groups* (London: Routledge, 1987).

Bob Dick, *Helping groups to be effective* (Brisbane: Interchange, 1991).

Em Griffin, *Getting together* (Downers Grove: IVP, 1982).

David W. Johnson and Frank P. Johnson, *Joining together: Group theory and group skills* (New Jersey: Prentice-Hall, 1975).

Hugh Mackay, *Why don't people listen?* (Sydney: Pan, 1994).

John Mallison, *The small group leader* (Adelaide: Open Book, 1996).

Trevor Tyson, *Working with groups* (Melbourne: Macmillan, 1989).

5. Helping people pray

Don A. Carson, *A call to spiritual reformation* (Grand Rapids: Baker, 1992).

Ole Hallesby, *Prayer* (Leicester: IVP, 1948).

Bill Hybels, *Too busy not to pray* (Leicester: IVP, 1988).

6. Sustaining group members

Gary Collins, *Christian counselling* (Dallas: Word, 1987).

Helena Cornelius and Shoshana Faire, *Everyone can win: How to resolve conflict* (Sydney: Simon and Schuster, 1989).

Lawrence J. Crabb Jr and Dan B. Allender, *Encouragement: The key to caring* (Michigan: Zondervan, 1984).

Lawrence Crabb, *Understanding people: Deep longings for relationship* (Melbourne: Interbac, 1987).

Gerard Egan, *The skilled helper* (Monterey: Brooks Cole, 1990).

Hugh Mackay, *Why don't people listen?* (Sydney: Pan, 1994).

Gail Sheehy, *Passages,* 2nd ed. (Sydney: Bantam, 1996).

7. Continuing as a leader

Eugene Peterson, *Working the angles* (Michigan: Eerdmans, 1987).